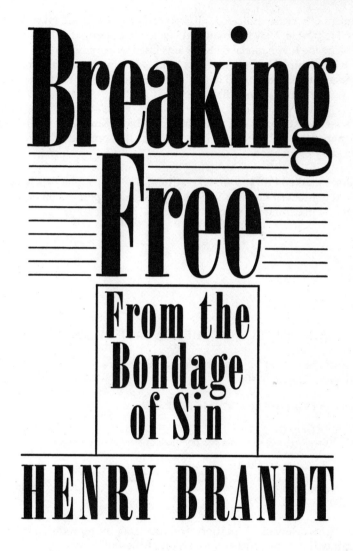

Breaking Free

From the Bondage of Sin

HENRY BRANDT

BREAKING FREE—FROM THE BONDAGE OF SIN

Copyright © 1994 by Harvest House Publishers
Eugene, Oregon 97402

Library of Congress Cataloging-in-Publication Data

Brandt, Henry R.
    Breaking free— : from the bondage of sin / Henry Brandt.
       p. cm.
    ISBN 1-56507-188-3
    1. Christian life—1060–   2. Sin.   I. Title.
    BV4501.2.B6857   1994   93-40122
    241'.3—dc20   CIP

Printed in the United States of America.

94 95 96 97 98 99 00 — 10 9 8 7 6 5 4 3 2 1

*To all the people who anonymously illustrated this book
by giving us a glimpse of their lives.*

With Gratitude

Kerry Skinner, Minister of Education at my home church, suffered through five or six drafts of these chapters with me. Without him, there would be no book.

My pastor, Dr. Keith Thomas, kept nudging me along by means of frequent conversations about the book.

Homer Dowdy, my longtime friend, an author himself, gave me invaluable help with chapters 6–9.

Steve Miller, my editor with Harvest House, handled the editing smoothly, professionally, and firmly. He has been an appreciative and friendly encourager.

Finally, my wife Jo kept the family details going so I had the freedom to write.

Contents

Before You Begin 7

1. The Ups and Downs of Life 11

2. How Thoughts and Feelings
   Can Hurt You 23

3. The Law of Sin 45

4. Overcoming the Law of Sin 61

5. The Hindrances to Self-Discovery 71

6. Sick or Sinful? 83

7. The Missing Link 93

8. How to Deal with Your Anger 109

9. Is There a Right Kind of Anger? 129

10. Dealing with a Child's Anger 141

11. Perfect Love Eliminates Fear 153

12. Enjoying the Spirit of Life in Christ 163

13. Finding Peace from Stress 175

14. Help for a Hard Journey 191

Notes 204

Before You Begin

Each year we pass through another Christmas season. I remember the time when the reason for the season was to celebrate the birth of Jesus Christ. His birth was recognized in the halls and classrooms of our educational institutions, government buildings, stores of all kinds, and in the minds of the vast majority of the people in our nation.

Why did Jesus come to earth to live among people, die on a cross, and rise again? "[To] save his people from their sins" (Matthew 1:21).

Jesus Himself gave us a sharp, clear word picture of some of the sins He saves us from: "For from within, out of men's hearts, come evil thoughts, sexual immorality, theft, murder, adultery, greed, malice, deceit, lewdness, envy, slander, arrogance and folly" (Mark 7:21-23).

After Jesus arose from the dead and just before He left for heaven, He instructed His disciples that their mission was to teach all nations how to deal with sin: "Repentance and forgiveness of sins will be preached in his name to all nations, beginning at Jerusalem" (Luke 24:47).

Doesn't it strike you as strange, then, that the word "sin" has almost completely disappeared from our vocabulary? Jesus Himself gave an explanation why this has happened:

> *Everyone who does evil hates the light, and will not come into the light for fear that his deeds will be exposed (John 3:20).*

In 1973, Dr. Karl Menninger wrote a book entitled *Whatever Became of Sin?* In it he noted that in 1953 (20 years before he wrote the book), President Eisenhower quoted Lincoln during his declaration of a day of prayer:

> It is the duty of nations as well as of men to own their dependence upon the overruling power of God, to confess their sins and transgressions in

humble sorrow, yet with assured hope that genuine repentance will lead to mercy and pardon.[1]

Dr. Menninger emphasizes that for the next 20 years, presidential declarations have eliminated any reference to sin. As a nation, he said, we officially stopped sinning after that declaration.

Menninger offers a reasonable explanation for people leaving "sin" out of their vocabulary. At the turn of the century, the use of the scientific method led to new theories of behavior and learning. Here are a few of them:

- *Messner* demonstrated that under hypnosis a person could be induced to do or think what he did not realize he was doing or thinking, nor remembers that he had done so.

- *Pavlov* and then *Watson* experimented [with considerable success] with ways of conditioning people to have a reflex response to a specific signal.

- *Freud* emphasized that understanding one's self better often leads to controlling one's self better. Examining the motivation behind your behavior is believed to have a certain enlightening or freeing effect. He asserted that a love/hate conflict toward relationships with partially buried, partially exposed memories should be labeled a neurosis and regarded as an illness.

- *Skinner* declared that what is believed to be voluntary behavior is actually predetermined by past stimuli.

- *Rogers* discovered that listening can relieve sufferers from doubt, anxiety, depression, phobias, and hysterical pain.

- *Menninger* declares that misbehavior has explanations other than sheer willfulness or aggressiveness.

- *The medical profession* prescribes mood-altering drugs that provide patients with a temporary escape from pain, anxiety, boredom, and remorse.

With all this "scientific" methodology there has come a wide departure from simple good/bad behavior. Physical problems are treated as a symptom for badness. There is an underlying disease for which the offender is not entirely to blame. Quoting Menninger:

> When the normal devices for tension management are not adequate to handle the stresses which develop or accumulate in our daily routines of life, there is a series of increasingly powerful emergency measures available which are automatically employed by the person. Many of these are physical, and if they become visible as "symptoms" they lead to medical attention and repair. But they may also be psychological symptoms.
>
> One man reacts to increased tension with a headache, another with high blood pressure, and still another with sleeplessness, irritability, and depression. On an empirical basis, these psychological reactions to overstress, these automatic emergency management devices, can be grouped into five levels or degrees of severity.
>
> ... It would take too long to list all of them, for they are many. They include such things as anger (one of the cardinal sins of old, you may remember) and depression, anxiety, and excessive day-dreaming. They include phobias and delusions and hallucinations. But they also include the bad judgment of drunken driving and the incorrigible impulsivity of child-beating, and the distress and pain of stomach ulcers. They include the desire to steal and obesity; they include bizarre sexual activities of various kinds; they include drug addiction and self-mutilation and check forging and convulsions—these, and many more.[2]

I see a mass movement in church circles toward the scientific method. People steadfastly resist the diagnosis of personal sin. It is much easier for a person to accept that his symptoms have some underlying pathology. They have a human or cultural origin, and the individual is likely not to blame for this condition. And there is no reason to turn to God;

it is a human problem caused by social interaction and it must be solved on a human level with the help of trained human beings.

This is the approach taken by the government, most educational institutions, most medical and psychological personnel, and by a rapidly growing number of church-related personnel.

An observer of the social scene must look on with growing alarm at the rapid increase in teen pregnancies, venereal diseases, sexual abuse, adultery, abortions, alcoholism, drug abuse, wife beating, stealing, fraud, deception, sexual or racial discrimination, poverty, material greed, family breakdowns, and blurred morals.

This book is a call for us to stop and locate ourselves. These problems surely involve the sinfulness of the individual. But with the scientific approach, sinfulness as a possibility is ruled out; it is not even considered.

A human approach does indeed relieve the symptoms. But there is no human remedy for the problem, which is sin. The cure is out of this world. Only God can help. Hopefully this book will help to illuminate the barriers (sins) that come between a person and the resources available from God through Jesus Christ.

Again, Jesus came to save us from our sins. If there is no human remedy for sin, should we not pause and take a careful look at the biblical definition of sin and its cure? God gave a clear assignment; we will give account.

1

The Ups and Downs of Life

---◆---

I had a lot to learn after I completed my university work. During my eight years of study, my wife and I lived hand-to-mouth in modest housing, had few clothes, and did our food shopping carefully.

After graduation I was just getting started as a teacher and counselor. A letter came from a rural Kansas town; inside was an invitation asking me to come for a week to lecture on a biblical view of mental health.

This town was surrounded by beautiful, rolling hills and lush, productive farmland. The air was fresh and clean. There was lots of sky above, and we enjoyed spectacular sunsets and beautiful moonlit nights. There were prosperous farmers who lived in large, lovely homes with all the conveniences anyone could ask for. They looked out of their picture windows at their oil wells pumping black gold 24 hours a day. Everyone had several big cars in their driveways and we ate sumptuous meals. Everyone was elegantly dressed. The church was beautifully furnished.

All this luxury bedazzled me. *Maybe I could afford a bit of this luxury soon*, I thought to myself, *after years of Spartan living.* You would think if there were any place in the world where people would be content and satisfied, it would be in this town. No doubt these people could teach me a thing or two about mental health.

To my surprise, I was swamped by people who requested counseling. There were many troubled hearts in those beautiful homes. People were lonely, worried, disillusioned, and fearful. Many of them tossed and turned in their comfortable beds and often wet their pillows with bitter tears. Human nature is the same wherever you go, and sad to say, luxury and plenty do not quiet the human heart. These people pleaded for me to tell them what to buy, or eat, or drink, or where to go, or what to do to find some relief from their tense, anxious bodies.

Beauty Without Peace

Della was from one of those lovely homes. She drove to my office in a fine luxury car. She was a beauty. Every hair was in place. The skillful use of cosmetics gave just the right touch to her complexion and eyes. A carefully chosen dress complemented her body. She was married to a handsome, hardworking husband. They lived in a roomy, nicely furnished house. They had one child and planned to have at least two more.

She had the same questions that I have heard repeated hundreds of times since. Della wondered, "I have everything I ever wanted. Why do I hurt? Why can't I relax?"

She had consulted a physician because she was experiencing occasional pain in the chest area and she struggled with a shortness of breath. After looking at the test results, her physician gingerly asked if she might be having any personal or family problems. He suggested that she consult a psychiatrist. She felt insulted, so she indignantly proceeded to get a second opinion. It was the same as the first opinion.

As this story tumbled out, it was easy to see that she was a tense, stressful young lady. She couldn't imagine why she needed a counselor. She had a good life and a good marriage. Why, then, did she have chest pains and shortness of breath?

I urged her to go home and think about the possible causes of her symptoms. Was there anything in her life that made her feel angry, resentful, bitter, or rebellious? She told me immediately that she had no such problems.

She left.

Della called me the next morning. "Could I come in?" she asked. "The sooner the better." She was ready for some help.

Apparently that night, after she had talked with me, she and her husband watched a football game with another couple. During the game, her husband yelled at the referee and argued loudly with his friend several times. Della didn't say anything, but by the time the game was over she was disgusted and embarrassed. Her husband sensed something was wrong, but she simply told him she was tired.

Della told me that she discovered soon after her marriage that her handsome, hardworking, fun-loving husband was also gruff, rude, and demanding. When he wanted to speak to her he would do so from wherever he was—even if he was upstairs in the bathroom and she was downstairs in the kitchen. He would shout loudly enough to be heard and expected her to reply immediately. If she didn't, he would come storming to her and give her an angry tongue-lashing for not listening to him. If he was watching a ball game on TV, he would cheer or boo or yell at the umpire as loudly as the people in the crowd at the stadium. During the evening news he would react loudly and give his opinions as though he were addressing an audience.

Yet when there were guests in the house he would speak in a conversational tone, so Della's friends had no idea what she endured.

She discovered that this was a family pattern. They were a loud bunch who turned down the volume when company came. While Della and her husband were courting she was company. Now that they were married, she was family.

Della was a soft-spoken person. She was accustomed to conversational-level talk. No one ever shouted in her family, especially from one room to another. Any effort on her part to get him to see her side of the issue was just brushed aside. After several tries failed to get him to at least discuss the problem, she gave up and never brought it up again.

I reminded Della about the words I asked her to think about the day before. We ended up agreeing that she deeply resented her husband's behavior and his total disregard for her style of communicating. Outwardly she was friendly, but last night she almost lost control. "He has no idea how I feel and couldn't care less," she said bitterly and burst into uncontrollable weeping. After she quieted down she said she felt as if a heavy load had been removed from her shoulders.

Finally she was able to admit to herself that her response to her husband was a miserable concoction of resentment, anger, hatred, and rebellion. To make matters worse, she covered it all over with behavior that made her look perfectly happy.

Here was a beautiful, perfectly groomed lady. She drove one of the finest luxury cars on the market. She lived in a spacious home that she helped to design and furnish. Her husband was a leader in the church.

But she was hurting with chest pains and had trouble breathing. She could not enjoy life because of a tiny word that has been banished from most people's vocabulary: *"sin."*

She was a prayer away from a solution. But repentance for sin is rare. Resentment, anger, hatred, and rebellion are sins. All she could see were the side effects: chest pains and shortness of breath.

Let's take a look at two Bible verses. Do either or both of them have any bearing on Della's problem?

> *"In your anger do not sin": Do not let the sun go down while you are still angry, and do not give the devil a foothold (Ephesians 4:26,27).*

> *Get rid of all bitterness, rage and anger, brawling and slander, along with every form of malice (Ephesians 4:31).*

The Battle for Your Mind

The body, host to the mind, can influence its invisible guest. I was reminded of this when traveling with a missionary friend in Africa several years ago. He was stricken with an attack of malaria. Over a period of several days this normally keen individual was frequently delirious. During this time it was impossible for me to discuss anything of a serious nature with him.

Most people need a given amount of sleep or they become irritable. The induction of a narcotic or alcohol into the body decreases the ability to think straight. Even food can affect the mental process—ask any luncheon speaker who has seen part of his audience drift off to sleep.

Though the body can influence a person's mind and his emotional state, medical science avers that the mind holds even greater mastery over the body.

The Mind Can Cause an Aching Body

To come to the decision that will lead you into the pleasant valleys of peace is to struggle with your own will. Let me illustrate this by noting the experience of Jerome Weller.

Weller was a department foreman at a manufacturing firm in Trenton, New Jersey. One day his boss called him into the office and said, "Jerry, as you know, things are a bit slow around here these days. I realize you have worked hard and run one of the best departments in the company. But my orders are to cut one supervisor, so I am letting you go."

Weller was stunned. He was the only Christian among the foremen. The other supervisory personnel, including his boss, liked to go out drinking and had some wild parties together. As a result, their work sometimes suffered and Jerry had to step in to rescue them. He had worked hard and now this was his reward.

Weller soon faced a financial slump. He had been making payments on a new home and a car but when his salary was suddenly cut off, he was in trouble. He lost both the house and the car and had to move in with his parents, who lived in Michigan. While with them, he had nothing to do but sit in a comfortable chair and mull over his experience.

"So this is the reward for hard work and clean living," he said to himself over and over. The more he thought, the more bitter he became. He found it hard to eat and harder to digest what little he did eat. He suffered from painful cramps. His physician told him that his condition stemmed from his emotions. But most of his friends reassured him that he had a right to have some emotional problems.

Twelve years later, time seemed to have healed the wound. Weller found another job and was quite successful in it. He was, in fact, the general manager of a manufacturing outfit with eight plants. One day while he was inspecting one of the plants, the personnel director asked him if he would like to meet the plant's new chief engineer. Of course he would, and did. Weller found himself face-to-face with the man who fired him 12 years before. Here working for him was the person who had caused him so much grief, pain, and embarrassment.

"I sure made a terrible mistake back then," the engineer said to Weller when they were alone. "Will you forgive me?"

"Oh, certainly. Forget it," Weller replied.

Jerome Weller said he would forgive, but within himself he nursed a gnawing bitterness toward this man. His stomach problem returned and he began reliving those confusing, painful days of long ago. He had thought this period of his life was long forgotten, but now he found himself fuming in his plush office, wanting only to get even.

One day he related the experience to me, then asked how one could work with a person who had treated him as this man had.

What would have been your reply?

God's Enabling Power

I pointed out several Scripture passages to Jerome Weller. One describes the work of the Holy Spirit:

> *But we have this treasure in jars of clay to show that this all-surpassing power is from God and not from us. We are hard pressed on every side, but not crushed; perplexed, but not in despair; persecuted, but not abandoned; struck down, but not destroyed. We always carry around in our body the death of Jesus, so that the life of Jesus may also be revealed in our body (2 Corinthians 4:7-10).*

The apostle Paul spoke here of trouble, perplexity, persecution, and rejection. All these had happened to him. But Paul also said there is a power that will enable a man to face such treatment without distress, despair, self-pity, or ruin. It is the power of God. I discussed this with Jerry Weller, but at the time it seemed to mean little to him. I then spoke of the end products of distress, pointing out that definite bodily changes are involved. "Your blood pressure, respiration, and digestion can be affected," I said.

"Are you suggesting that I am my own problem?" he asked. "Are you saying that you would have acted differently had you taken what I took?"

I assured Jerry he was his own problem and reminded him of one of Jesus' statements: "But I tell you who hear me: Love your enemies, do good to those who hate you, bless those who curse you, pray for those who mistreat you" (Luke 6:27,28). This, I said, could be his attitude toward the man who had fired him.

Jerry became furious with me. How could I be so lacking in sympathy and understanding? Now he was upset not only at the engineer, but at me as well.

Who was Jerry hurting when he carried his grudge around within himself? Who was affected when he sat in his chair in Michigan and seethed over a man who wasn't even in his presence? Himself, of course.

There is a power that will enable you to face your circumstances without distress. It is the power of God, made available to you through the dying of the Lord Jesus. God's power—and His alone—can make you want to forgive a person who has misused you. But Jerome Weller did not want to forgive that engineer; he wanted to get even.

Jerry argued that he had a right to be bitter. I agreed he did and I would agree with anyone who stoutly stood on his right to be angry and unforgiving over a wrong done to him. It is your privilege to be upset and miserable. But as long as you insist on retaining your misery, you will have it.

The mere knowledge of sin, however, does not eliminate it or the problems that it causes. Wise is the person who heeds the advice of the apostle James:

> *Do not merely listen to the word, and so deceive yourselves. Do what it says. Anyone who listens to the word but does not do what it says is like a man who looks at his face in a mirror and, after looking at himself, goes away and immediately forgets what he looks like. But the man who looks intently into the*

perfect law that gives freedom, and continues to do this, not forgetting what he has heard, but doing it— he will be blessed in what he does (James 1:22-25).

The exhortation here is to people who want to be free from their misery, who want to be lifted out of their sin. But wasn't it strange that my counselee, who said he wanted relief from his upset condition, became all the more upset because I told him he did not need to be upset? One would think he would have seized the opportunity to shed his spirit of bitterness and hate.

For many people yielding bitterness and hatred in exchange for a tender heart toward someone who doesn't deserve it would not be a blessed relief but rather a great sacrifice. Like Jerome Weller, untold numbers of people would like to be free from their aches and pains. But if you say that means they must relinquish a long-standing grudge, they say they would rather ache.

There in Jerry's nice walnut-paneled, softly lit office we were locked in a struggle. If I had told him that his grudge was normal and that I probably would have acted the same way, he might have enjoyed some relief, but the inner sore would have continued to fester and spread its poison.

A Willingness to Yield

The only solution is for a person to quit fighting and turn to God for a spirit of love toward someone who does not deserve it. And when you yield, the problem is nearly over. The Bible says it is your move: "Come to me, all you who are weary and burdened, and I will give you rest" (Matthew 11:28).

One day, Jerry Weller finally did turn to God for help with his bitterness and hatred. Today his digestive disorder is no more; his aches and pains are gone. He is at peace with himself and with the man who had abused him. Jerry is enjoying God's peace, the fruit of the Spirit, in his life.

How does this change come about? *By confessing or acknowledging that you have done wrong—that you have sinned.* David wrote this about his sin: "Then I acknowledged my sin to you and did not cover up my iniquity. I said, 'I will confess my transgressions to the LORD'—and you forgave the guilt of my sin" (Psalm 32:5).

When Jerry paid attention to and took care of his own reaction to the other man's sins instead of concerning himself with what the other man had done, he found himself on the road to peace.

To see your sin is disturbing only if you fight what you discover. If, instead, you admit it and seek help from God, the result is not guilt but an overwhelming sense of forgiveness, cleansing, renewal, and peace.

The pathway to spiritual peace is a struggle. Discover the truth about yourself and you will naturally shrink from it; become offended and defensive and you will be bound in the strong fetters of your sin. What a difference you will find if you just heed the promise of Jesus: "If you hold to my teaching, you are really my disciples. Then you will know the truth, and the truth will set you free" (John 8:31,32).

Indeed, this is one of the mysteries of life: Why can't intelligent, educated, prosperous people get along?

It was 1944 when this question first came to my attention. World War II was raging. Most men of my age were in military service. I was deferred because I had some tool engineering experience. I was needed in the production of war materials.

Everyone knew someone who was touched by an injured or a killed family member. Whenever a soldier died, the military would send the family a small cloth banner. On the banner was a gold star on a purple background. The family would hang this banner in one of the windows of their home. As the war progressed, more and more houses had a gold star in a window.

The times were conducive to serious heart searching. The suspense in the air was very real. When out in public, people huddled into little groups and were very likely trying to make sense out of the times. They were anxious, nervous, restless. Tempers flared. Tears came easily. Tensions developed quickly in families, at work, and among friends.

I was no exception; but, I had found the key to taming my temper, which flared up too often at home and at work. The Bible held the key for me; all I needed to do was make the choice to accept it as truth.

My wife and I tried desperately to help numerous people who had similar problems to mine. We saw constructive change in dozens of people who turned to God for help as I had done. We concluded that the Bible contained the most important information in the world: It had an accurate understanding of human nature.

In the fall of 1944 my wife and I and our two preschool children headed for Houghton College in New York. Our quest was to learn what the Bible had to say about interpersonal relations. And we put our trust in a guarantee from Jesus Himself: "Heaven and earth will pass away, but my words will never pass away" (Matthew 24:35).

2

How Thoughts and Feelings Can Hurt You

◆

D r. S.I. McMillen, a much-respected and loved physician, taught the college Sunday-school class at the church we attended. He gave a series of lectures on how certain thoughts and feelings can cause pain in many parts of the body.

Dr. McMillen used some visual aids and pamphlets authored by Dr. O. Spurgeon English of Temple Medical School and sponsored by Sandoz Pharmaceuticals to illustrate his lessons.

Up to this time, I had always assumed that pain meant something was wrong with the body and that a physician would know how to fix it. The proper choice of pills or an injection will hopefully do the job. It simply never occurred to me that thoughts and feelings could affect the body.

Dr. McMillen introduced me to a new term, "psychosomatic," which has to do with a physical disorder caused by or noticeably influenced by the emotional state of the patient.

How Emotions and Thoughts Can Affect the Heart

When I was growing up, I often heard the heart referred to as a "ticker." When there was a problem you simply got it fixed, much like you would take your broken watch to a jeweler.

According to Dr. English, the emotional state of a person can cause a perfectly healthy heart to beat faster and irregularly. There can be the sensation of tightening, pain, and numbness. There can be a shortness of breath and the feeling of faintness, weakness, or giddiness. There can be an "all-gone" feeling and profuse perspiration. The patient may feel like falling in a heap.

How Emotions and Thoughts Can Affect the Digestive System

The words that follow explained some of the mysterious aches and pains I had experienced prior to my attending Dr. McMillen's Sunday-school class. This information was news to me but not to the physician. I quote:

> For decades it has been known that a personality problem that cannot be solved by the mind itself is prone to be "turned over" or "taken up" by some other part of the body. When an irritating friend or a troublesome family member cannot be coped with, the patient becomes "sick," he can't "stomach" it, or it "gripes" him. The physician

knows that the cause of these gastrointestinal disturbances is emotional conflict. He knows it is the attitudes of generosity and responsibility struggling with an opposing wish to escape them.

Laboratory tests show that under emotional stress changes in glandular activity occurs in the mucous membrane and various parts of the digestive tract. Not only does the blood supply change markedly, but secretions of various types increase or decrease in an abnormal manner. Changes in muscle tone in the digestive region can occur, causing painful cramps.[1]

How Emotions Can Affect the Skin

The skin is well supplied with blood vessels, nerve endings, and glands. Many common verbal expressions in use today reflect an unwitting acceptance of the connection between a person's emotions and thoughts and his skin.

- Blush with shame
- Itching for a fight
- Burn with indignation
- Pale with fright
- Irritated beyond words

The Autonomic Nervous System

The Sunday-school lesson that interested me the most was the one about a function of the body that I had never heard of before: the autonomic nervous system.

There are certain emotional centers in the brain that are linked to the entire body through the autonomic nervous system. This system can be compared to the wires that carry electricity from a main power source to all the outlets in your house.

Charges of emotions are relayed from the brain, down the spinal cord, and through the autonomic nerves to the blood vessels, muscle tissues, mucous membranes, and skin. So when you are under emotional stress, all parts of your body can be subject to physical discomfort because of a change in blood nourishment, glandular function, or muscle tone.

For example, a speaker who is about to be introduced before a crowd oftentimes is fearful over facing the audience. Suddenly his mouth will become dry. That's because his blood vessels have constricted and glandular activity has reduced. When the fear goes away, the dryness will also go away.

It has also been proven that emotional stress will increase the size of the blood vessels in your head; this, in turn, produces pain because of the stretching of the tissues around the blood vessels and the consequential pressure on the nerve endings.

Dr. English wrote a list of the thoughts and feelings that can disturb the autonomous operation of the body:

envy	self-centeredness
frustration	hostility
worry	need for approval
oversensitivity	guilt
ambivalence	repressed hostility
inferiority	anxiety
fear	sorrow
ambition	rage
resentment	

Dr. McMillen gave us a list of words that were very similar. This list, called "the acts of the sinful nature," came from the Bible:

> *. . . sexual immorality, impurity and debauchery; idolatry and witchcraft; hatred, discord, jealousy, fits of rage, selfish ambition, dissensions, factions and envy; drunkenness, orgies, and the like (Galatians 5:19-21).*

Don't Be Alarmed

We all know about smoke alarms or burglar alarms. Did you know your body has been marvelously equipped with alarm systems?

When you are healthy, the heart does its work. The stomach does its work. We take it for granted that our arms and legs will respond when needed. The brain does whatever brains are supposed to do. The body simply operates in autonomous (self-regulating), painless silence when it works properly.

But when you are injured or ill, you know it. A sore muscle cannot be ignored. Neither can indigestion, a fever, a sore throat, a headache, a speck in your eye, or a sliver in your finger. The pain or discomfort must be recognized and addressed.

The Body Sounds a Sinful Alarm

Bob was a young pastor fresh out of college and just beginning seminary. He wanted to do well in his first church staff position. Bob had always wanted people to accept him and approve of what he said and did. However, not long into his new job, he discovered that not every church member liked what he said and did.

Bob began to notice that reading caused tremendous pain in his eyes. Normal lighting in his office gave him headaches. He couldn't sleep at night. He was not as relaxed as he once was. Sitting still was almost impossible. Nervous twitching compelled him to see a Christian medical doctor. Bob was convinced that he had a brain tumor.

After the examination, the doctor said to him, "Bob, the good news is that you don't have a brain tumor. The bad news is you have a severe case of stress! I will recommend two solutions to your problem and you can decide which one you want to try. I can give you tranquilizers to help you relax; or, you can leave my office, spend time with God, and ask Him to show you why you can't relax."

Bob left the doctor's office knowing what he needed. He told himself that he respected the judgment of the people who did not approve of all he said and did. But he resented them and tried to cover it up in their presence. This was self-deception. The result? Restlessness and sleeplessness.

Bob's experience illustrates these biblical principles:

> *For it is not the one who commends himself who is approved, but the one whom the Lord commends (2 Corinthians 10:18).*

> *If anyone would come after me, he must deny himself and take up his cross daily and follow me (Luke 9:23).*

After Bob repented of his hypocrisy and allowed the Lord to give him genuine respect for the people he once despised, the headaches, nervous twitching, and all the other symptoms were completely gone within a week.

Like the red warning light on the dashboard of a car, Bob's body warned him that not all was well with his spiritual life. I can share other examples with you:

One day during a counseling session Charles Reed spoke of his problem at home. Often he would arrive in a good mood and would be hungry enough to eat a side of beef. Then his wife would begin to air her complaints. Perhaps he had slammed the door when he came in. Or, he might have been a few minutes late. So just before dinner was ready, his body would become tense and he would lose his appetite. His angry, resentful reaction to his wife produced drastic bodily changes.

A young girl that reported she suffered from severe headaches. Careful questioning disclosed that the headaches always occurred when her fiancé failed to call when he said he would. A further look back through her life showed that she had headaches whenever something went wrong with her plans. She also resented anyone who interfered with her plans.

Eddie Bond sought counseling at the recommendation of his physician. "How can you help me get over a stiff neck?" he asked, truly puzzled. As he told his story, it became clear that life, to him, was one big pain in the neck. The tenseness of his neck muscles gave him the pain. He was tense because he approached the problems in his life as if he were a football lineman charging his opponent. He had a quick temper.

Mrs. Frick was a beautiful, cultured, well-educated woman. But in certain situations she was having difficulty swallowing her food. I learned that these times of difficulty came in connection with appointments that her husband demanded she make and keep. She resented his demands; she actually could not "swallow" them.

The Bible acknowledges the connection between certain feelings and bodily affliction. For example, King David was aware of the relationship between sin and pain: "Because of your wrath there is no health in my body; my bones have no soundness because of my sin. My guilt has overwhelmed me like a burden too heavy to bear" (Psalm 38:3,4).

Psychosomatic Problems

My first encounter with a person who had a psychosomatic problem came early in my career as a professional counselor. A young minister from another state, about 1,500 miles away, called me. He had a painful, bleeding ulcer. Some local physicians told him that the cause had to be emotional problems. A thorough checkup at the Mayo Clinic confirmed the local diagnosis. He had visited a counselor and now understood his problem. But now he wanted to discuss it with me. Would I be willing to see him? I agreed to do so, but his request seemed strange since he understood his problem.

He took charge during the first three appointments. He said that since he had some psychotherapy already, he would brief me on what he had learned. He described some conflicts that were taking place between himself and his family. I tried to get a word in occasionally, but he brushed aside my efforts and kept on talking. During the third meeting he described his past conflicts with teachers and coaches.

Finally, I decided on a way to stop him. I simply said, "Stop."

He stopped. I asked, "Do you know what you are doing?"

"Yes," he replied, "I know what I am doing. I'm afraid of you. I wanted to come here; but at the same time, I dreaded coming. I don't understand it."

"You said you came because you have a bleeding ulcer and your physicians tell you that your pain has an emotional cause. Is that what you said?"

"That's what I said. My stomach has been in knots ever since I arrived."

Even though he came 1,500 miles to get help, he didn't seem ready to face up to the real issues. I showed him a chart developed by Dr. English that shows how emotional stress can cause physical discomfort because of a change in blood nourishment, glandular function, or muscle tone. Dr. English says that when we can't cope with a troublesome person, we say we can't "stomach him." This, in turn, can be the reason for disorders of the digestive tract.

I asked the young minister one question: "Who are you mad at?"

He couldn't think of anyone. I urged him to observe himself the rest of the day and night and see if he could discover any emotional reactions between now and the next appointment.

He came to the fourth appointment. This time he sat down and was quiet. I asked him what he had found out about himself. This was his story:

He came from a quiet little mountain town. No one was in a hurry there. A driver could approach an intersection slowly, look around, and take his time going through. Well, you can't do that in Detroit (the location of the appointment). Here, people are in a hurry. When he left my office, he drove as if he were back at home. He eased up to a stop sign and was greeted by the horns of two cars behind him. Both drivers passed him and expressed their disapproval with hand signals as they passed. My client became furious. Then it dawned on him that he was very angry at some people he had never even met.

That night he was eating a meal in a restaurant and a customer was seated at the table next to him. The other person kept sniffling and blowing his nose; he must have had a bad cold. My client became increasingly annoyed as he listened—so much so that he got up and left half of the meal on the plate. As he left, he became conscious of that familiar knot in his stomach.

After he shared about these incidents, we had no problem agreeing that he had been angry at the drivers and the restaurant customer. We also had no problem agreeing that anger was a work of the flesh or a sin (Galatians 5:20).

Then he quoted a verse: " 'In your anger do not sin': Do not let the sun go down while you are still angry, and do not give the devil a foothold" (Ephesians 4:26,27).

The young minister said that in his anger he had not sinned, but rather, that he was being "righteously indignant." (This was my first encounter with that term.) He assured me that he had thoroughly studied this verse in seminary, and that his experience yesterday clearly came under the heading of righteous indignation. He claimed that his response to the drivers and the man in the restaurant was a normal, healthy response toward unreasonable, impolite behavior.

So then I asked, "What else could be troubling you? Do you have any problems in your little mountain town that arouse your righteous indignation?"

He said yes; there were two deacons at his church who "upset" him.

At seminary, he had learned how a good Sunday school should be organized. When he came to this church, he saw immediately that the Sunday school needed changing. He also learned in seminary that people learned more by means of the "eye gate" than the "ear gate." He was eager to use this information to show the church why the Sunday school needed reorganization. He made charts so they could *see* the need as well as *hear* the need. The time came to make the presentation. The church was gathered. He stepped up to the podium armed with his charts. He was excited. After he made his presentation, the man who was the acknowledged leader of the church got up to speak.

The young minister was shocked when he heard what the leader had to say: "I have been in this church for over fifty years, and I don't see any need to change our Sunday-school program."

The reorganization was voted down. The young minister was livid with rage. He qualified this anger as "righteous indignation" because this man had blocked the improvement of the Sunday-school program.

In seminary, the minister also learned how important music was to a worship service. The music in his church was sadly lacking, so he made a proposal to improve the music. Again, a "pillar of the church" arose and declared the present program adequate. The young minister's proposal was voted down. Again he "hit the ceiling."

He was furious over a righteous cause!

In both instances, of course, he claimed to maintain a proper pastoral manner. Outwardly, he accepted the church's decisions. Inwardly, he boiled over the two men. He could feel his stomach knot when he got up to preach. These men were always present and he had to greet them at the door after the service, using his best pastoral manner.

That wasn't all, but I will not go into the unresolved issues between him and his wife.

It seemed clear to me that this dear pastor was consumed with anger. He was desperately desirous of being a Spirit-filled leader of his people. It was equally clear to me that he was denying a condition within himself and suffering the consequences. I reluctantly and uneasily called a few verses to his attention:

> *A malicious man disguises himself with his lips, but in his heart he harbors deceit. Though his speech is charming, do not believe him, for seven abominations fill his heart. His malice may be concealed by deception, but his wickedness will be exposed in the assembly (Proverbs 26:24-26).*

> *He who conceals his sins does not prosper, but whoever confesses and renounces them finds mercy (Proverbs 28:13).*

> *But if you harbor bitter envy and selfish ambition in your hearts, do not boast about it or deny the truth. Such "wisdom" does not come down from heaven but is earthly, unspiritual, of the devil. For where you have envy and selfish ambition, there you find disorder and every evil practice (James 3:14-16).*

As gently as possible, I urged the minister to consider the application of these verses to his condition. It appeared that he was denying an enormous amount of anger, which manifested itself as a disorder of the digestive tract. The pressure of the knot in his stomach was like making a fist and squeezing his hand with all his might. It hurt. He could relieve the pain immediately by relaxing the hand.

His response was, "Have you ever been a minister?"

"No sir, I have not."

"I thought so," he retorted, obviously disturbed. He rejected my statement that his anger was sin. In fact, his face flushed as he responded with anger toward me. We both agreed there was no doubt that his response was anger. He had expected me to support him in his response to the men at church and to his wife; instead, I was now added to the list of people who "upset" him.

I asked him to listen to James 3:17,18: "The wisdom that comes from heaven is first of all pure; then peace loving, considerate, submissive, full of mercy and good fruit, impartial and sincere. Peacemakers who sow in peace raise a harvest of righteousness."

He then asked, "Do you mean to tell me that you would have acted any differently if you had been in my place?"

"If I were in your place and responded like you did, that would make us both wrong," I answered. "If we are sinful, that's good news. That's the simplest problem there is if it's only sin. Jesus died to cleanse us from sin. And as a result, we now have access to the wisdom that is from above."

I asked him to ponder these verses and see what happened. He stomped out of my office without another word. There I sat, wondering, *Dare I approach a minister this way?* All I could do was cling to my faith in what the Bible said.

Later he came in for a fifth appointment. I was quite apprehensive as I saw his car come into the parking lot. As he got out of the car, I hardly recognized him. He stood straight, a twinkle in his eye; he looked relaxed. I wondered what had happened to him, and he was quick to let me know.

After his last visit he was livid with rage at me, he said. At the same time, the knot in his stomach became unbearably painful. He then was forced to concede that if this was the result of righteous indignation, he had better try something else. He could not deny the condition of his body. It dawned on him that perhaps his indignation was not the righteous kind after all. He was alienated from his wife, from the two lead deacons in his church, and from me. He was suffering physical pain which had been diagnosed as psychosomatic by the best of physicians. The ceiling seemed to be as far as his prayers went. Finally he saw the light at the end of a dark tunnel.

He began to pray: "Father, there is hatred and anger and self-seeking in my heart. There is confusion. It's been a long time since I've experienced a peaceable, gentle, merciful spirit willing to yield to others. I have been hypocritical. Yes, it's true. Wash me clean. Restore my soul."

Afterward he fell asleep. It was daylight again when he awakened. The knot in his stomach was gone. He sensed an attitude of thankfulness toward me and a feeling of respect and appreciation toward his deacons. He sensed an affection for his wife that he had not known in a long time. He was free at last. Let me tell you, that was a holy moment for both of us!

That day I realized more clearly than ever that I need to trust the Bible, declare it as I see it, and *depend on a client's second reaction rather than the first.*

I cautioned him to take it one day at a time and to be vigilant and discerning about where his wisdom came from. He took off for his church in that tiny mountain town. We kept in touch for several years, and he reported that his experience lasted. In fact, he was able to see other sins in his life that he took care of. Now he was able to deal with problems in and out of his church with wisdom that came from above instead of with painful, supposed "righteous indignation."

He was the first of hundreds of righteously indignant Christians who ended up in my office. They came because their physicians ruled that their headaches, stiff necks, skin problems, chest pains, breathing difficulties, digestive problems, and tensions were caused by emotional stress. And unfortunately, theologically trained, highly respected staff people from the churches they attended had justified the symptoms by attributing them to righteous indignation.

How Sin Affects the Body

Since 1944 I have been pondering this issue: Are we sick, sinful, or both when we hurt? Medical researchers have recently expressed the opinion that destructive emotions are caused by a chemical imbalance in the body. But I ask the question, is it possible that a chemical imbalance in the body could have been caused by destructive emotions? It seems obvious to me that since sin is so easily cleansed, the presence of sin should be explored first.

A pastor questioned me about this issue. Someone in his congregation had suffered from severe anxiety attacks. His physician prescribed a drug that corrected the problem. After three years of treatment, it was clear that the patient was fine as long as he took his pills. Was I implying that the cause of these attacks was sin? (I had used the term "destructive emotions.") I asked him, "Shouldn't everyone be open to the possibility of sin in their lives?"

Later that day I was chatting with several people. A man interrupted our conversation. He wanted to talk to me immediately. He seemed disturbed, and paced the floor while he waited.

When we were finally able to talk, he wanted to know if I thought that anxiety was caused by sin. I replied that we can be both sick and sinful at the same time. I told him that if he cared to make an appointment, I would be pleased to talk with him more. We set a time and he left in a huff. When we met again I reviewed his reason for wanting to see me. He said he was on medication for stress and that it solved his problem. I then asked why he wanted to see me. He seemed abrupt and annoyed, and then it dawned on me. This is the man that the pastor asked about—the one who had been under treatment for three years.

I asked if he wanted to explore his spiritual life. Yes, he did.

I asked if there were any tensions in his marriage, family, church, or at his children's school. His answer each time was a testy no almost before I finished the question. I remarked that he couldn't possibly have given any thought to my questions. He admitted that was true, so I chided him for brushing off my questions. He left, again in a huff.

The next time we met, he seemed lighthearted and radiant. He decided I had been right. He had been nursing some nasty grudges in his heart, but now he had given them up. His wife wondered what happened; she hadn't seen him so cheerful in a long time. Clearly, his response to the people he held grudges against—bitterness, resentfulness, anger—was sinful, and repentance brought immediate relief. Whether or not he was also sick was a matter for his physician to determine.

You may be thinking that to explore the possibility of sinfulness is a harsh approach. If so, be assured that most people I talk with think the same as you do. Let me simply remind you that Jesus came to save us from our sins, and that if your problems are linked to sin, you are just a prayer of repentance away from wholeness and restoration. Is it not heartless cruelty to treat people for sickness if they are only sinful? When a Christian is suffering bodily affliction, exploring the possibility of sinfulness should have priority.

A Patient's Perspective

A dear woman named Mrs. English asked me for an appointment. I was reluctant to do so because it appeared to me that she was merely sick and in need of a physician. She later wrote a tract about our experience together; it is a startling illustration of the interplay between sickness and sinfulness:

> PAIN with a purpose!
> Fighting for my life! That's what I was doing. Pain creeping through my body had progressed from aching hips to aching spine, both knees, now one ankle. A horrible nightmare, but I was living it!
> In 1967 x-rays revealed the discomfort in my hip was osteoarthritis. Within two years the hurt had traveled over almost my entire body and I was frightened and appalled at what lay ahead.
> In late 1969 I went to a very fine specialist. He ordered x-rays and blood tests and, then announced that although I did have arthritis, the pain was too severe to be caused only by my physical condition. I left his office in a daze. Getting into the car, I pled, "Lord, if these pains are psychosomatic, I need to know." It was very perplexing for supposedly I was a happily married woman with her needs met, one who had no real excuse to worry and who claimed

her trust in God meant that, through Him, she could be joyful, loving, peaceful, gentle, and good. But I wasn't. Active in Christian circles, I was regarded as a "nice, sweet lady." But I wasn't.

For the next three days I felt much better and again went to the Throne of Grace and said, "Father, You have healed my body but how about my mind?" That evening someone disappointed me. When I went to bed my bones felt as though they had been lit with matches. This was so devastating that I fell on my knees and cried, "Help!"

An eminent Christian psychologist was coming to town in February of 1970 and a one hour interview was arranged. I prepared for it by reading his book *The Struggle for Peace* and by compiling a list of "what bugs me." A pattern began to emerge as I read and made my list—every time I did not get my own way, I had adverse reactions!

As my counselor read the list I told him of my nasty feelings and reactions, admitting hatred for the way I felt and acted, but being unable to prevent it. He dropped a bombshell! He said I was an angry person, that I like being an angry person or I would have changed long ago.

I could hardly believe it—but I had no choice. I was fighting for my health. So I took it on faith that I was in the right place at the right time, listening to the person God had sent to help me out of this mess.

The doctor further explained that I had fooled many people, including myself, making them think I was what I should be. "The heart is deceitful above all things and desperately wicked; who can know it?" [Jeremiah 17:9 KJV]. I was denying what was in the inner recesses of my life and thus was in great conflict. Galatians 5:17 describes it well.

By now I was in tears, recognizing that actually it was a question of violating a divine principle of spiritual living, just as someone who is sick has broken some medical rule of living. I couldn't wait to hear what would come next because I was looking for a way of escape.

As I continued to cry my heart out, my counselor pointed me to answers from the Bible: "He that covereth his sins shall not prosper: but whoso confesseth and forsaketh them shall have mercy" [Proverbs 28:13 KJV]. Going from Scripture to Scripture he showed me the way out.

I confessed my sin and received forgiveness for my reactions. Since that day I have asked that I might not yield to the temptation to strike back at anyone, but prayerfully ask Him to take away these feelings and fill me, by His Spirit, with love, joy, and peace. Then I remind Him that I am thankful that He is so gracious, kind and good to me. He is always so gentle yet firm in His corrections.

I could hardly believe what happened. My severe joint pains were relieved, blood pressure was down, a new ability to relax developed, my first reaction was not always [that] of anger. He began filling me by His Spirit with a new kind of peace and joy and a capacity to love.

Was it real? More than two years have elapsed since my visit to the Christian psychologist, and I feel better now than then. I have come to know the Lord Jesus Christ more intimately, to appreciate the work of the Holy Spirit in my life as never before and to trust God for all things in a way unknown in the past. Each new day I look forward to increased spiritual growth.[2]

A Doctor's Perspective

Dr. S.I. McMillen spent many years studying Jewish and Christian writings in search of biblical principles and directions for living. As a result of this research he wrote the bestseller book *None of These Diseases*, which describes the physical consequences of wrong living. He pointed out that there may be sin in the picture when aches and pains show up:

> Peace does not come in capsules! This is regrettable because medical science recognizes that emotions such as fear, sorrow, envy, resentment and hatred are responsible for the majority of our sicknesses. Estimates vary from 60% to nearly 100%. Emotional stress can cause high blood pressure, toxic goiter, migraine headaches, arthritis, apoplexy, heart trouble, gastrointestinal ulcers, and other serious diseases too numerous to mention. As physicians we can prescribe medicine for the symptoms of these diseases, but we cannot do much for the underlying cause—emotional turmoil.[3]

In his book, Dr. McMillen gives a masterful description of the effects of hate:

> The moment I start hating a man, I become his slave. I can't enjoy my work anymore because he even controls my thoughts. My resentments produce too many stress hormones in my body and I become fatigued after only a few hours of work. The

work I formerly enjoyed is now drudgery. Even vacations cease to give me pleasure. I may be in a luxurious car that I drive along a lake fringed with the autumnal beauty of maple, oak, and birch. As far as my experience of pleasure is concerned, I might as well be driving a wagon in mud and rain.

The man I hate hounds me wherever I go. I can't escape his tyrannical grasp on my mind. When the waiter serves me porterhouse steak with French fries, asparagus, crisp salad, and strawberry shortcake smothered with ice cream, it might as well be stale bread and water. My teeth chew the food and I swallow it, but the man I hate will not permit me to enjoy it. . . .

The man I hate may be many miles from my bedroom; but more cruel than any slave driver, he whips my thoughts into such a frenzy that my innerspring mattress becomes a rack of torture. The lowliest of the serfs can sleep, but not I. I really must acknowledge the fact that I am a slave to every man on whom I pour the vials of my wrath.[4]

When your body hurts, check your spirit. The pain may be a signal to pay attention to your thoughts and emotions.

I once assumed that pain was always the physician's territory. But now I ask, When resentment, anger, hatred, and rebellion are involved, are you not in the minister's territory?

Here is a scripture to think about: "So I say, live by the Spirit, and you will not gratify the desires of the sinful nature" (Galatians 5:16).

3

The Law of Sin

◆

W hy are we prone toward anger, jealousy, hate, and vengeance? The apostle Paul says there is a law at work within us: "But I see another law at work in the members of my body, waging war against the law of my mind and making me a prisoner of the law of sin at work within my members" (Romans 7:23).

Seeing and Hearing the Invisible

In grade school I learned about an invisible law called gravity. It was at a playground where eight swings were installed side by side. We had a contest to see who could make his swing go the highest. I was standing up on my swing and at a point where it was as high as it could go and I slipped—and I kept on going up and clear out of sight.

Do you believe that? No, thanks to the law of gravity, I came down so hard the impact broke a tooth.

Wouldn't it be difficult if gravity worked only part of the time? Imagine walking and never knowing for sure whether you would fly up or come down. But fortunately we can depend on the law of gravity. And though you can't touch it, if you jump out of a window, you will feel it.

Scientists work with invisible matter they call "atoms." They tell us that the things we see are made up of things we can't see.

In junior high I saw a demonstration of this. The school I attended had several temporary classroom buildings. They were made of wood, stood one story high, and were set up on cement blocks. If you were small enough, you could crawl underneath. One windy day, some burning paper blew out of a trash burner nearby and it landed under one of those wooden buildings. There were some dry weeds under the building. They caught fire and ignited the wooden floor. Before anyone discovered the fire, the building was a blazing inferno. Fortunately this happened in the evening when there was no one in the building. We watched it burn; the fire gave off intense heat. It had gotten such a start that the firemen just let it burn and concentrated on protecting the other buildings. There were books, clothes, and desks that ended up as a pile of ashes.

I can remember my amazement while watching so many different things turn into a pile of ashes. I looked at my shirt, my shoes, my baseball, our house, and our furniture, and marveled that these things which I can see and touch are held together by some invisible power and that the application of fire could turn them into mere ashes.

You would not say, "I don't believe germs exist" just because you can't see them. Once I had malaria. I couldn't see what caused my aches and pains, but there was no denying that they were real.

These invisible powers work according to predictable laws. We can chart a course by the stars. Day follows night, and so on. This is an orderly world.

The Law of Sin at Work

People interact according to predictable laws as well. There is a law that describes one side of every person; it is called the law of sin:

> *I know that nothing good lives in me, that is, in my sinful nature. For I have the desire to do what is good, but I cannot carry it out. For what I do is not the good I want to do; no, the evil I do not want to do—this I keep on doing. Now if I do what I do not want to do, it is no longer I who do it, but it is sin living in me that does it. . . . What a wretched man I am! Who will rescue me from this body of death? Thanks be to God—through Jesus Christ our Lord! So then, I myself in my mind am a slave to God's law, but in the sinful nature a slave to the law of sin (Romans 7:18-20,24,25).*

There is a tiny word tucked into these verses that you seldom hear these days. The word is—should I say it?—*"sin."* These verses define the term "sin" to mean the breaking of God's law. An equally important concept to understand is the "law of sin." It is one of the most important of all laws to understand because it will determine your future conduct.

A knowledge of sin and what to do about it is the most important information in the world, and the Bible is the source of that information. Almost all the people who talk to me about themselves have little or no knowledge about the Bible. It follows that they also have little or no knowledge about sin.

Della is an example. She is a beautiful woman, well-groomed, fashionably dressed, and a delightful person to talk to. I am convinced that she wants desperately to be an easygoing wife. She wants to overlook her husband's faults. She wants to be a kind, considerate, even-tempered mother. She has succeeded in *acting* the way she would like to be, but she is unable to *be* who she wants to be. Her husband's ways stir up unbearable hostility within her. So far she has managed to swallow it, but the result is pain in the chest area and shortness of breath. She yells at her child. She illustrates this law of sin: "I have the desire to do what is good, but I cannot carry it out" (Romans 7:18).

Della assumed that her symptoms meant she was sick. She was shocked and indignant when her physician found no sickness. She thought he must be incompetent. The physician then told her to see a psychiatrist. To her dismay, the second opinion was the same. The psychiatrist offered her a prescription that would help her to relax.

In my presence Della reluctantly admitted that anger, resentment, and rebellion were deep within her. Dare we call it sin? Doesn't she get any credit for trying to be nice? What about her husband? Isn't he the cause? These are serious questions. Is she sick, sinful, or both? She left to think about it.

I have heard hundreds of similar stories. People begin by saying, "I have everything I always wanted and

I'm doing everything right!" But the same gnawing emptiness and repetitive questions remain:

- Why am I restless?
- Why am I worried?
- Why am I tense?
- Why do I hurt?
- Why am I uncomfortable?
- Why am I disturbed?
- Why am I nervous?
- Why am I unhappy?
- Why am I under stress?

I am convinced that like Della, all of us sincerely want to overlook other people's faults and be easygoing, loving, generous, cooperative, and sacrificial. But something holds us back. Could it be this law of sin? Paul seems to say yes: "For what I do is not the good I want to do; no, the evil I do not want to do—this I keep on doing. Now if I do what I do not want to do, it is no longer I who do it, but it is sin living in me that does it" (Romans 7:19,20).

I listened to a fine-looking man tell me that he finds himself withholding kind words for his wife and blurting out a nasty criticism instead. He drags his feet when an act of kindness could be done toward her, but is quick to insist that she carry out a selfish request for him.

It is usually the unexpected circumstances that give you an unexpected glimpse of yourself. Joe considered himself to be an easygoing, friendly person. He liked his work and got along well with his associates. Then his boss got transferred. The new boss rearranged Joe's workplace, changed his secretary, and gave him some new duties that he didn't like. Joe changed from being a cheerful, cooperative person to a disgruntled, rebellious employee. He hated the new boss. His inner response to the new superior resulted in behavior that missed his own personal standard of conduct.

This is the law of sin at work. It suggests a conflict between the desire to do good and the inability to do it.

The Bible sums up this condition very simply: "Anyone, then, who knows the good he ought to do and doesn't do it, sins" (James 4:17).

Perhaps you have been present with someone who has eaten too much and is confronted by a luscious dessert. With fork in hand he declares, "I shouldn't eat this." Then he deliberately proceeds to do what he just declared he shouldn't do—eat the dessert.

Another Bible verse describes this type of struggle: "For the sinful nature desires what is contrary to the Spirit, and the Spirit what is contrary to the sinful nature" (Galatians 5:17).

Positive Aspects of the Negative

The law of sin usually becomes obvious when we interact with other people. Though we may desire harmony with others, a law comes into play that hinders our cooperation. This is the reason so many people are unhappy and there is so much conflict between individuals. The Bible pinpointed the trouble long ago: "Each of us has turned to his own way" (Isaiah 53:6).

Each person likes his own ideas, plans, aspirations, and longings. This is true for everyone. Thus when you encounter resistance to your wishes, or face demands that are not to your liking, the tendency is to rebel, to attack, to run, or to defend yourself. The natural reaction is to be resentful, bitter, stubborn, full of fight. It is easy for you to think that your desires are the reasonable ones. A person will find a way to make a selfish drive seem selfless, deceiving even himself.

Furthermore, it is natural to shrink away from an honest glimpse of yourself. To back off from reproof is as human as shielding the eyes from a burst of light in a dark room. Again, the Bible's assessment of the heart—that it is deceitful above all things (Jeremiah 17:9) and that men love darkness rather than light because their deeds are evil (John 3:19)—is as up-to-date as the literature on psychology that describes the mental mechanisms for evading the truth.

The patterns of deceit and self-defense are so systematized that their names are common dictionary words: rationalization, regression, suppression, repression, extroversion, introversion, compartmental thinking, and projection. To peer further into the darkness, such avenues can lead to psychoses requiring hospitalization—or to broken homes, crime, vice, or even murder or suicide.

Such is the heart of man. One shudders to contemplate its potential for evil. The Bible and literature on psychology alike paint this oppressive picture.

Scripture's Accurate Diagnosis

But as already mentioned, there is hope. Since we are looking to the Bible as our guide, we can turn to it not only for a description of man as he naturally is, but for the path to peace from our disturbances, neuroses, and psychoses. Psalm 119:165 says, "Great peace have they who love your law, and nothing can make them stumble."

Many people turn to a counselor for help because they are in circumstances that offend them or have caused them to stumble. They are dissatisfied, irritated, unhappy. Either they flee from the vexing situation or attack it. One would think that people would rush to buy a book that pointed out the path to peace and the way from offense to freedom. People do buy it—millions of copies every year. The Bible continues to be the all-time best-seller. But it is a book that most people quickly lay aside because it reproves and corrects. Man simply does not like the truth that he discovers about himself in the Bible.

The Problem of Sex

Galatians 5:19 says that two acts of the sinful nature are sexual immorality and impurity. You may recall when Magic Johnson, one of the greatest basketball players of all time, said he had an announcement to make. There he stood, in superb physical condition, a wholesome smile, admired by many, wealthy, a successful businessman and athlete. He recently married his college sweetheart. They were expecting their first child. He had it all; a truly magic career. But then he announced that he was retiring from basketball immediately because a medical test revealed that he had contracted the HIV virus—AIDS.

The nation was stunned. All that many would say was that he took the news with courage, grace, and dignity. The sad fact is that our magic hero had so many sex partners he lost count. And now he is paying the price of ignoring a biblical one-liner: *"avoid sexual immorality"* (1 Thessalonians 4:3).

Mary Fisher had wealth, power, and knowledge—a combination that some people mistakenly perceive as sure protection against AIDS. But Fisher, the daughter of multimillionaire, financier, philanthropist, and presidential confidante Max Fisher, knows better. In July she tested positive for HIV, which causes AIDS.

She contracted the virus through her marriage to artist Brian Campbell. They divorced in 1990, but she cannot be freed from paying the price for her husband's infidelity. Allow me to cite another biblical one-liner: *"You shall not commit adultery"* (Exodus 20:14).

The William Kennedy Smith rape accusation trial captured newspaper headlines all across the country for days. His accuser did not prove her case, but the trial brought up the issue of sexual immorality. Mr. Smith went into a bar and met this lady for the first time. They drank and danced together for several hours, and at 3:00 A.M. they went to the Kennedy estate. They had sex together on the lawn at 4:00 A.M. Easter Sunday. *The only issue at the trial was whether the act was rape.* They couldn't even remember each other's names. Ironically, his lawyer called this incident "an act of love." Heaven help us!

On prime-time TV I watched a show hosted by Peter Jennings. One feature of the program was a demonstration of how to use a condom properly. I remember when the subject of sex was discussed in a whisper; today, it's prime-time material.

The law of sin draws people toward sexual misuse. In a marriage relationship, satisfying the sex urge is one of life's most pleasant experiences. The process is exciting and pleasurable. But the end result of practicing adultery and fornication is fear, guilt, embarrassment, broken hearts, disease, pregnancy out of wedlock, poorly matched and early marriages, divorce, and death.

In Florida, Governor Chiles reports that there were 28,000 teen pregnancies in 1991. The state spent $796 million to support these families. He says that 85 percent of teen parents drop out of school. They are seven times more likely than their peers to spend the rest of their lives in poverty.

The fastest growing HIV-infected population in Florida is the 20–29 age group, which means that many of these young adults were infected in their teens. An 11-member panel on AIDS reported 5,499 new cases in 1992. They propose that condoms be made available in public schools and that teens be taught the correct way to use them. They added that students should also learn that it's okay to abstain.

Dear reader, you are looking at the results of the law of sin. Imagine, a panel on AIDS apologetically declaring that it's okay to abstain from sexual activity!

Even people who are not actively involved in adultery or fornication may struggle with feelings, desires, and thoughts about sex. Jesus recognized this problem when He said, "Every man who looks at a woman lustfully has already committed adultery with her—in his heart" (Matthew 5:28 PHILLIPS). Our Lord was referring to mental adultery, an invisible power that tears marriage partners apart, causes trouble between parents and children, between families, and in churches.

Because this is an invisible condition, its presence between people is difficult to detect. And it's common for this condition of the heart to be fueled by pornographic material.

Scripture is clear on the issue of immorality: *Sexual activity outside the bounds of a married couple (male and female) is a sin against God.*

The Problem of Annoyance

Galatians 5:20,21 says that "hatred, discord, jealousy, fits of rage, selfish ambition, dissensions, factions and envy" are works of the lower nature. Other words that we could use would be quarreling, debate, disunion, and anger. I am going to lump all of these together and call them "annoyance."

Feelings of annoyance can range all the way from very slight annoyance that you hardly notice to intense annoyance that breaks through our shells and causes our faces to flush, our hearts to pound, and causes our bodies to break into a sweat. Annoyances can cause us to say things we later regret, hit someone, or refuse to associate with someone.

Slight annoyances are cumulative. They can happen all day long. For example, at breakfast you find that your coffee isn't quite hot enough. At work the boss asks you to do something you don't like to do. Some of your fellow workers tell a joke that you don't like. You call your wife and the line is busy. There is a traffic jam on the way home. What a relief to get home! Then your little child wants to climb on your lap when you want to read the paper. You tell your child to get down but he persists. Finally you get up and give the child a savage spanking, all out of proportion to what was done. You are releasing the tension that has built up over a period of time because of a whole series of little annoyances. And while an adult can yell at or spank his child and get away with it, he cannot yell at his boss without suffering immediate consequences.

There is an invisible power within you that is turned loose when annoyances accumulate—a power that turns you into a blazing inferno of unpleasant emotions and causes you to say, feel, think, and do things that you normally don't do when you are calm. Families, friends, churches, and nations are often torn apart by the invisible power of hatred, malice, anger, strife, and wrath.

Remember Della? She placed a high value on self-control. As a result she behaved beautifully on the outside but was miserable on the inside. Jesus, addressing the religious leaders of His day, said, "On the outside you appear to people as righteous but on the inside you are full of hypocrisy and wickedness" (Matthew 23:28).

An apt description of this inner condition that plagues everyone was written by a scientist named Henry Drummond, who lived in the last century:

> We are inclined to look upon bad temper as a very harmless weakness. We speak of it as a mere infirmity of nature, a family failing, a matter of temperament, not a thing to take into very serious account in estimating a man's character.
>
> The peculiarity of ill temper is that it is the vice of the virtuous. It is often the one blot on an otherwise noble character. You know men who are all but perfect, and women who would be entirely perfect, but for an easily ruffled, quick-tempered, or "touch" disposition. This compatibility of ill temper with high moral character is one of the strangest and saddest problems of ethics.
>
> No form of vice, not worldliness, not greed of gold, not drunkenness itself, does more to un-Christianize society than evil temper. For embittering life, for breaking up communities, for destroying the most sacred relationships, for devastating homes, for withering up men and women, for taking the bloom off childhood; in short, for sheer gratuitous misery-producing power, this influence stands alone. . . .
>
> Analyze, as a study in Temper, the thundercloud itself as it gathers. What is it made of? Jealousy, anger, pride, uncharity, cruelty, self-righteousness, touchiness, doggedness, sullenness. In varying proportions, these are the ingredients of all ill tempers.

You will see then why Temper is significant. It is not in what it is alone, but in what it reveals. This is why I take the liberty now of speaking of it with such unusual plainness. It is a test for love, a symptom, a revelation of an unloving nature at bottom. It is the intermittent fever which bespeaks of unintermittent disease within; the occasional bubble escaping to the surface which betrays some rottenness underneath; a sample of the most hidden products of the soul dropped involuntarily when off one's guard; in a word, the lightning form of a hundred hideous and un-Christian sins. For a want of patience, a want of kindness, a want of generosity, a want of courtesy, a want of unselfishness, are all instantaneously symbolized in one flash of Temper.[1]

The Problem of Drunkenness

Let's look at one more problem: drunkenness. I am asked this question quite frequently: "We are confronted increasingly by the demands socially to drink alcoholic beverages. Many of our friends tell us how harmless drinking is and yet our church emphasizes how dangerous it is. We would like your comments." Let me quote the Bible:

> *Listen, my son, and be wise, and keep your heart on the right path. Do not join those who drink too much wine or gorge themselves on meat, for drunkards and gluttons become poor, and drowsiness clothes them in rags. . . . Who has woe? Who has sorrow? Who has strife? Who has complaints? Who has needless bruises? Who has bloodshot eyes? Those*

*who linger over wine, who go to sample bowls of
mixed wine. Do not gaze at wine when it is red,
when it sparkles in the cup, when it goes down
smoothly! In the end it bites like a snake and poisons
like a viper. Your eyes will see strange sights and
your mind imagine confusing things. You will be like
one sleeping on the high seas, lying on top of the
rigging (Proverbs 23:19-21, 29-34).*

The danger of drinking alcoholic beverages has been
recognized for centuries. Seneca, an ancient Roman
writer, philosopher, and statesman, said, "Drunkenness
is nothing but voluntary madness."[2] Bertrand Russell
(1872–1970), a British philosopher, mathematician, and
social reformer said, "Drunkenness is temporary suicide."[3]

From the standpoint of the person who drinks,
there is some value: a sense of comfort, relaxation, and
temporary relief from the irritations and frustrations of
life. Yet the Bible clearly says, "Do not get drunk on
wine, which leads to debauchery. Instead, be filled with
the Spirit" (Ephesians 5:18).

Yes, there are two ways you can look at alcohol. You
can look at it sparkle in the glass and enjoy it as it
goes down your throat. It can calm you down and give
some temporary relief. Or, you can recognize that a little
drinking all too frequently leads to more drinking, which
in turn can bring about negative consequences.

At the close of 1992, law enforcement officers for
my county in Florida issued a report. It gave the total
statistics of drunk-while-driving arrests. In my county
there were 2,596 arrests, an average of seven per day. The
youngest drunk was age 15, and the oldest was age 92.

There were 66,876 arrests statewide—about one for every 300 licensed drivers.

Many of these DUI drivers are riches-to-rags stories. They are literally on the edge with financial difficulties, they have problems at work, their spouse leaves, and the next thing you know, they are arrested DUI.[4]

This report reminds us that there is a great need for people to find some relief for their restless, anxious bodies. It's true that alcohol offers that relief quickly. But in the process, people end up in greater trouble than what they faced originally.

It was Shakespeare who exclaimed, "Oh, God, that men should put an enemy in their mouths to steal away their brains."

Drunkenness is a sin against God.

4

Overcoming the Law of Sin

◆

My local newspaper reports the consequences of the law of sin every day. Of course the tragedies reported are not called "sins." A quick glance at the paper (*Palm Beach Post*, February 2, 1993) as I write this chapter chronicles some of yesterday's activities:

- Two teens rape mom, kill two daughters, shoot mom

- Florida legislature ready to redeem itself from last year's unseemly and unproductive political battle

- A woman is beaten every 15 seconds daily in this country; two to four million women are physically assaulted every year

- Tabloid reporter guilty of defrauding employer by creating fake names to use as news sources

- Serb-Croat war resumes after lull

- Judge Wachter, one of the most influential judges in the country, charged for a $20,000 extortion payment demand from ex-lover

- Aspen businessman confesses fatal stabbing of his wife and starvation death of 18-month-old daughter

- Bobby Humphery (pro-football player for the Miami Dolphins) charged with assault and possession of cocaine

The breakdown of the family, the rise in crime, physical and sexual abuse, violence, deception in business and government, and drug abuse all reflect sinful behavior.

Doctors, psychologists, government officials, and educators all agree that the human heart must be tamed. And almost all the people in these fields start from the premise that the solution to these problems depend on human intelligence, the scientific method, and social and cultural interaction. There is no deity to save us. There are no fixed standards to go by. We must help ourselves.

Some theologians and Christian laypeople (I am one of them) depend on faith in a living God. Our problems are the result of deviation from His standards, otherwise called sin. We cannot help ourselves. We need a change of heart as a starting point. God has made provision for such a change; it will unfold as you read on.

Do you realize that only God can help you harmonize your actions with your inner life? If we could help ourselves, then Jesus died in vain. Quoting again from the Bible:

> *What a wretched man I am! Who will rescue me from this body of death? Thanks be to God—through Jesus Christ our Lord! So then, I myself in my mind am a slave to God's law, but in the sinful nature a slave to the law of sin* (Romans 7:24,25).

Two more biblical one-liners come to mind: *"He [Jesus] . . . will save his people from their sins"* (Matthew 1:21 PHILLIPS), and *"Repentance and forgiveness of sins will be preached in his name to all nations"* (Luke 24:47).

A Resistance to the Truth

Some churches are criticized because their ministers upset people when they preach about the sinfulness of man and the inflexible standards of the Bible. Once I had a long conversation with a fellow counselor about the value of "deeper-life" conferences, during which the details of the ideal Christian life are discussed. He felt very strongly against these types of conferences. He believed they did irreparable damage because after each such conference a wave of very upset people came to him. They were greatly disturbed because no matter how hard they tried, they could not attain perfection.

People have often turned to me as a counselor because their pastor has upset them. After listening to him preach about sin, they feel guilty and inadequate. They were much happier people before they began attending church, studying the Bible, and facing the truth. Therefore, could it not be reasonable to conclude that their problems were caused by what they heard and read? To remove the cause would seem the logical way to relieve the person's anxiety. And this has long been advocated. There is widespread pressure on ministers to preach "positive" messages and to emphasize the good in man.

Wait just a minute, though. Perhaps a look at the methods of another profession may help you understand the value of pointing out the bad, the evil, the negative.

It Is Positive to Deal with the Negative

Consider the physician. As he diagnoses you, he has only one basic question: "What's wrong?" This is certainly a "negative" approach!

If 99 percent of you is in good health, your doctor is interested in only the 1 percent of you that is not. If you have an infected fingernail and the rest of you is healthy, he concentrates on the fingernail. If you have a pain in your abdomen, he does not overlook the abdomen. Instead, he examines it thoroughly, even if the examination brings you additional pain.

Why do you put up with such treatment? Because the doctor's objective is to restore your health. He eventually eliminates sickness and may save you from death by subjecting you to great pain and even the risk of your life on the operating table. It is positive to eliminate the negative. It is healthy to eliminate disease. It is good to eliminate evil.

The Need for an Accurate Diagnosis

A neighbor in seemingly good health went to her physician because she developed a slight pain. An investigation revealed a tumor and abdominal surgery was called for. The doctor's announcement of what was needed not only upset the woman, but her whole family and some people in the neighborhood as well. Why would a man want to subject this fine woman to such an ordeal? Why didn't he give her a sedative to help her forget the pain? Then no one would have gotten upset. But instead of prescribing a painkiller, he sent her off to a hospital, where her surgery confined her for weeks.

Think of the effect the doctor's diagnosis and prescription had on the woman's husband, their children, and their budget. But not a single person condemned the doctor. Quite the contrary, they were all grateful to him. They were appreciative of this person who had delivered such drastic, disturbing news and who had subjected the woman to the pain of a knife and her husband to such great expense. He would have done her a disservice to have acted otherwise.

The diagnosis did not depend on the notions of the physician, but on the condition of the patient's body. The doctor could not be guided by what the patient wanted to hear; rather, he had to follow the course of his findings. How does a person make the announcement of the need for major surgery a happy occasion? There is no way. What's important is that the proper diagnosis be made and the patient be told. The patient will get over the shock of the announcement; my neighbor did. Then it was up to her whether she would submit to the prescribed treatment. She could have tried to ignore the pain, kept busy, and attempted to forget about her condition. She might have tried to kill the pain with medication. The other alternative was to accept surgery, which she did.

An accurate diagnosis of a physical ailment is a matter for the physician. But the patient's future health is really his own decision.

To miss the mark of perfect health is common, but to deny that you are sick or to give up the quest for health is foolish. Wisdom calls for trying to discover the cause of your ill health—for the physician to give an accurate diagnosis despite the guilt, anxiety, or worry it might cause and for you to follow through on the doctor's advice.

No more steaks, desserts, or smoking is tough medicine even if it is presented in a tender, loving fashion.

The Need to Diagnose Sin

Now back to the point that ministers are pressured to emphasize the good and the positive because talk of sin and the negative is upsetting and causes anxiety and worry: Of course, the knowledge of sin produces such results. But your present comfort is of little value if there is, in fact, sin in your life. To diagnose sin, however disturbing it may be, is a positive act.

Your minister, counselor, or friend cannot determine what the diagnosis will be. I cannot determine what my client brings to me. If there is selfishness, touchiness, irritability, stubbornness, rebellion, hatred, or deceit within you it simply is there. I didn't put it there, but it is my responsibility to point out its presence. This may be upsetting to you, but I have found no other way to cure the problem. I have never known a person to discover the sin that was causing his trouble by my dwelling on his good qualities. And I have never found a way of pointing out a man's sin to him that makes him clap his hands with glee at the news. Jesus Christ emphasized this when He said of sinners: "You refuse to come to me to have life" (John 5:40).

Jesus also explained why people feel condemned and guilty: "This is the verdict: Light has come into the world, but men loved darkness instead of light because their deeds were evil" (John 3:19).

This is why people become disturbed when they

hear a minister of the gospel preach on God's standards for man. The Bible throws light on their conduct; it exposes their souls. The truth is often offensive, even if it is shared in a tender, loving fashion. When you are confronted, do yourself a favor and pay attention to the message rather than the manner of the messenger. The messenger may not be following his own advice. But if it is the truth, you would be wise to follow it.

Some Pharisees and teachers of the law asked Jesus why His disciples broke the traditions of the elders. For example, they didn't wash their hands before they ate. This is part of the Lord's response to them: "What goes into a man's mouth does not make him 'unclean,' but what comes out of his mouth, that is what makes him 'unclean'" (Matthew 15:11).

The disciples came to Jesus and asked if He knew that the Pharisees were offended by His answer. Jesus replied: "Leave them; they are blind guides. If a blind man leads a blind man, both will fall into a pit" (Matthew 15:14). Then Jesus added:

> But the things that come out of the mouth come from the heart, and these make a man "unclean." For out of the heart come evil thoughts, murder, adultery, sexual immorality, theft, false testimony, slander. These are what make a man "unclean"; but eating with unwashed hands does not make him "unclean" (Matthew 15:18-20).

A communications major would say that Jesus' handling of this dialogue was abrupt and harsh. A modern-day psychology major would say Jesus' answer was simplistic. They would say people with these problems are not unclean; their hearts are corrupted by society.

Though the words of Christ offended His listeners, their response did not change the truth He spoke. And herein lies tremendous hope. You may not be able to control what your wife or husband, father or mother, or anyone else says or does. You may not be able to change your environment. Yet Christ *can* cure you of the things that defile you from within. And this is good news because you can be changed. But you must decide whether to let God change you. If admitting you are wrong is the first step toward a great cure, why would you want to avoid it?

The Battle with the Will

To come to the decision that will lead you into the pleasant valleys of peace is to struggle with your own will.

Remember, as we learned earlier, an awareness of sin does not eliminate it or the problems that it causes. The apostle James encourages us with this advice:

> *Do not merely listen to the word, and so deceive yourselves. Do what it says. Anyone who listens to the word but does not do what it says is like a man who looks at his face in a mirror and, after looking at himself, goes away and immediately forgets what he looks like (James 1:22-24).*

How does this change come about? By confessing or acknowledging that you have done wrong, that you have sinned. David wrote this about his sin: "Then I acknowledged my sin to you and did not cover up my iniquity. I said, 'I will confess my transgressions to the LORD'—and you forgave the guilt of my sin" (Psalm 32:5).

To see your own sin is disturbing to you only if you fight what you discover. If, instead, you admit it and seek help from God, the result is not guilt but an overwhelming sense of forgiveness, cleansing, renewal, and peace. The Scripture states it this way: "Through Christ Jesus the law of the Spirit of life set me free from the law of sin and death" (Romans 8:2).

The pathway to spiritual peace is a struggle. Discover the truth about yourself and you will naturally shrink from it. If, however, you become offended and defensive, you will remain in the strong fetters of your sin.

What a difference you will find if you heed the promise of Jesus: "If you hold to my teaching, you are really my disciples. Then you will know the truth, and the truth will set you free" (John 8:31,32).

5

The Hindrances to Self-Discovery

◆

The first step toward peace is to discover yourself. The second is to square up with the truth
you find.

You will get fleeting glimpses of your true self (and
sometimes a very clear picture) as you interact with other
people, as you read the Bible, and as others minister to
you.

Yet the average person usually resists facing up to
his faults. Quite likely he will reject anyone who points
out his error. Jesus Christ gave the precise explanation
for this reaction when He said, "Everyone who does evil
hates the light, and will not come into the light for fear
that his deeds will be exposed" (John 3:20).

We possess a natural dislike for rebuke. We have a
built-in resistance to seeing our shortcomings. We react
to reproof as we react to pain. The tendency is to shrink

away, to protect ourselves from what we wish were not so.

Studying the Bible is a sure way to get at the truth about yourself, but it takes some effort, and no one can force you to study it.

King David said of God's Word, "Your word is a lamp to my feet and a light for my path" (Psalm 119:105). The apostle Paul wrote that "through the law we become conscious of sin" (Romans 3:20). And it was Jesus who commented, "Blessed rather are those who hear the word of God and obey it" (Luke 11:28).

Facing the Unpleasant Truth

As the truth about you emerges from some probing stimulus, you will either face it directly or turn from it. You will mellow or harden, depending on what you choose to do about your discovery.

A young couple came for counsel.

"How is it that at times we can be so cooperative, so tender toward each other, and 15 minutes later so opposed, so hostile, so cold?" asked Marvin, the husband. "How is it possible that we can pray together and feel united in our faith but then we are battling each other over an unexpected issue?"

Marvin then opened the door on their lives to afford a glimpse inside. He remembered the day he and Gloria, his wife, had driven to the city hospital and parked. As they glanced up to the eighth floor, Marvin breathed a prayer for their three-year-old son, who hovered between life and death. "Dear God, we love our boy and we want him, but may Thy will be done. Help Gloria and me to be worthy parents and give Jimmy a happy home."

At that moment Marvin and Gloria felt closer to

each other than at any time in their lives. Carefully he helped her out of the car; arm-in-arm they walked to the door and made their way up to the boy's room. Jimmy was asleep. A solution of some sort was being fed from a bottle into his arm. The parents looked at their son and their hearts beat as one for him. Marvin felt that he could never speak harshly to the boy again, that he could know no selfishness toward his son.

Jimmy recovered. What joy for Marvin and Gloria to bring him home! But after a week, the feelings Marvin experienced at the hospital had changed. In fact, antagonism toward both his wife and son crept into Marvin's heart.

The boy had been waited upon night and day in the hospital. After he arrived home, Gloria kept up the pampering.

"When are you going to let him grow up?" Marvin asked his wife.

One evening Jimmy was playing on the floor near the sofa where his parents were reading. He asked his mother to go into the next room and fetch his favorite truck. She put down her magazine and started to get the toy.

"Let him go for it himself, Gloria," Marvin said.

"I don't mind getting it for him," she replied.

Marvin nearly exploded. "You're spoiling him rotten! All he needs to do is point a finger and you jump."

Dad insisted that the boy get the toy himself. The child begged and pleaded and began to whine. Gloria became increasingly uncomfortable. Finally she defied her husband and got the truck. Jimmy was happy, but his father was enraged.

After Jimmy went to bed, a silence developed between the parents. Marvin felt quite justified for having taken his stand. Gloria felt Marvin was being too strict. While in the car outside the hospital and by their son's bedside they had shared the tenderest of feelings and identical goals. But now they were at complete odds.

Marvin and Gloria needed to face up to a biblical truth: "Each of us has turned to his own way; and the LORD has laid on him the iniquity of us all" (Isaiah 53:6).

The couple responded negatively: "Are you calling us sinners?" They found it hard to face the truth, even though they were fully aware that their behavior was inconsistent. They knew they were both missing the mark that they had agreed to aim at.

Sin Stands in the Way

Marvin and Gloria left the counseling session assuring each other of their devotion to a happy marriage. They renewed their vows never to fall short again. But they were soon back. They couldn't inspire each other to be consistent.

The apostle John wrote in his first epistle:

> *If we refuse to admit that we are sinners, then we live in a world of illusion and truth becomes a stranger to us. But if we freely admit that we have sinned, we find God utterly reliable and straight-forward—He forgives our sins and makes us thoroughly clean from all that is evil. For if we take up the attitude "we have not sinned," we flatly deny God's diagnosis of our condition and cut ourselves off from what He has to say to us (1 John 1:8-10 PHILLIPS).*

"But we are Christians," they pleaded. "What can we do?" John wrote:

> *I write these things [which give you a true picture of yourself] . . . to help you to avoid sin. But if a man should sin, remember that our advocate before the Father is Jesus Christ the righteous, the one who made personal atonement for our sins (1 John 2:1,2 PHILLIPS).*

You must be careful with the word "sin"; you must be sure of its meaning. Romans 7 defines sin as the inability to do the good you want to do; it is the drive within you that causes you to do what you don't want to do (verses 14,15,19).

Marvin and Gloria have moments when both of them agree that they are violently opposed to each other. Yet when they try to face the truth, they deny it and attempt to reassure each other that all is well. But it isn't. They want peace, but they fight the process that leads to peace. They fail to take advantage of one of the important benefits of marriage—the means that marriage provides for self-discovery. Because the tendency is to fight against such discovery, many find marriage distasteful. They do not like to be reproved, even if the criticism is true.

Everyday Living Exposes the Soul

The same holds true regarding work, social, and church relationships. The story of George Lund illustrates the point.

George wanted to clear up the gnawing sense of anxiety and growing unhappiness that plagued him, and hoped to do so before anyone else found out about his condition. So he quietly sought professional counseling. He would rather have died than have his associates learn that he was bored with church and its activities, dissatisfied with his wife, and annoyed with his fellow employees at work.

But the counseling experience was a shattering one. The counselor, who George suspected was a non-Christian, pressed him to share his antagonisms, and George did not like it. He insisted he had no antagonisms. He stoutly maintained that since he was a Christian he loved everyone and was nice to all. Still the counselor probed, and finally George blew his top.

Afterward he was ashamed because he had been a poor example of what a Christian ought to be. The counselor pointed out that George was filled with anger and hatred toward people rather than filled with love.

Then George came to see me. He was confused. Was he a Christian or wasn't he? He had asked God to help him show love to everyone. "Ever since this counselor forced me to blow up," he said, "I've been nasty to a lot of people." What evil thing, he wanted to know, had the counselor done to him?

What had the counselor done? He had led George to face the truth about himself. What truth? That he was an angry man with hatred burning in his heart toward the people with whom he worshiped at church, the people he worked with at the office, the members of his own family, and now, the counselor who, he maintained, had caused him to blow his top.

Because George pretended to be a happy man, he wanted to believe that he was one. Since becoming a Christian, he had always acted politely to everyone. His annoyances were his own secret. He controlled himself for the sake of his testimony. The psalmist described the behavior of such a person: "His speech is smooth as butter, yet war is in his heart; his words are more sooth-ing than oil, yet they are drawn swords" (Psalm 55:21).

Pretending to be happy didn't make George so. He was only being true to human form. Again, "The heart is deceitful above all things and beyond cure. Who can understand it?" (Jeremiah 17:9).

George Lund's emotions—his heart—told him he was a nice, loving, happy man. But he refused to recog-nize the deceit of his heart. What the counselor had done was to expose George to himself and lay open the false-ness of his heart. He made George see that his smooth, soft words covered a bitter war raging inside, that they sheathed the swords of hate and malice.

George might have discovered this truth for him-self. Like the fever that warns that all is not well in the body, the gnawing sense of uneasiness in his relation-ships with others ought to have made him aware that all was not well between him and the people in his life. But George did the natural thing—he disregarded the symp-toms, denying the truth. He could not admit to himself that there was anything in his heart but love.

Christians know they have a high and noble stan-dard to measure up to. Non-Christians may settle for a less-exacting standard. They know that if they fail, every-one else fails as much as they. So why not relax instead of trying to change the world? But for Christians, God's stan-dard allows no bitterness and strife. Therefore, if a believer becomes aware of bitterness and strife deep within, he can either deal with it, or simply put on a facade.

George was proud of his acting ability. "Usually I control my anger," he said. "Don't I get any credit for that?" His ability to act lovingly toward others presented an impressive testimony; but it did not satisfy him. As he became aware that he was only acting, the truth shook him up; he began to lose the control that he had held so tightly.

"I'm confused. Why doesn't God give me peace?" he asked. Look at what the Bible says about a person who lets sin lurk in his heart: "Your iniquities have separated you from your God; your sins have hidden his face from you, so that he will not hear" (Isaiah 59:2).

Repentance is rare. One tends to defend himself. Time after time George insisted he was an innocent man. He said the fault lay with the conduct of the people around him, including the counselor who goaded him. Nevertheless, the facts of his case contradicted him. His iniquities separated him from God and denied him peace from God.

"The counselor egged me on," George said repeatedly, reminding me that the flare-up was not his fault. Then one day he admitted that maybe he did lack love for certain people. But if he did, he asked petulantly, why didn't God give it to him? Now he blamed God for his anger.

When you get a glimpse of your true nature, your inclination will probably be to dodge the truth. But be aware that when you deny what you find in the recesses of your life, anxiety and unhappiness will slowly envelop you in their tentacles.

Fifteen-year-old Gene described himself as easy to get along with. But he came for counseling because of his hair-trigger temper. He had been thrown off the football team for fighting. One time at home when his mother demanded that he study instead of going outside to play baseball, Gene became so incensed that he threw his ball through the picture window.

When I asked him about this display of temper, he

dismissed any responsibility for it with a shrug. "Oh, I only get mad with my mother," he said. "Anybody would around her."

"What about the fights you get into at school?" I asked.

"Well, if you had been in my place, you would have punched those people, too. Anyone with guts would have. You would defend yourself, wouldn't you?"

Gene was a self-willed boy. He had no friends because they refused to put up with his lack of consideration and his quick fists. In spite of all the facts, Gene still insisted that he was an easygoing fellow. He really believed it; he was unhappy that others did not.

Repentance Is Rare

Fred Crompton came to my clinic because he was suffering from exhaustion. He was busy as a deacon in the church, made weekly calls on Sunday-school absentees, served on the counseling team of the citywide youth rally, and headed the planning committee of the local Christian businessmen's organization. Fred hardly ever missed a meeting at church. He also played tennis once a week and faithfully followed his son's high-school sports career.

Why wouldn't so active a man wear out? Yet his doctor could find no physical cause for his complaints.

In talking with him I learned that a year before, a trusted partner had cheated Fred out of his half of a business. I also learned that the demanding schedule Fred now followed had started about the time of his loss. Fred had no explanation.

"I've got the time to do the things I have always wanted to do," he said. "I'm glad I can do them."

"You mean you are thankful that you lost the business?" I asked.

"I had committed the business to God," he replied. "The Lord gives and the Lord takes away."

"Were you as busy in the partnership as you are now?" I asked.

"Oh, busier. I was a workhorse."

"Did you get exhausted then?"

"Not at all."

"Now you aren't as busy as you were before, but you are on the verge of a mental and physical breakdown. How do you explain that?"

He couldn't.

I asked if he still had contact with the man who had cheated him. He replied that their paths crossed occasionally.

"We see each other. I hold no hard feelings at all toward him."

"What was your reaction toward him when you first learned that he had cheated you?" I inquired.

"Must we go into that?" he asked, quite annoyed. "The incident is past. I have forgiven him. Let's forget it!" It seemed to me that Fred Crompton was getting hot under the collar. At least the flush of his skin indicated that he was certainly disturbed.

In later interviews it became clear that Fred was carrying a grudge against his former partner. He hated to admit it, but he was a deeply bitter man. Rather than face his reactions to an injustice, Fred had tried to bury them in a flurry of activity. Though he maintained a good front outwardly, the inward decay had pushed him to a point of near-collapse.

How sad. He was spoiling his own health because someone else did something wrong!

Why would anyone punish his own body with a seething, angry, hateful grudge when it can be removed and replaced with love, joy, and peace in exchange for a prayer of forgiveness and repentance?

The reason? Because the person is not convinced his anger is a personal sin. Instead, it is the result of someone else's errant behavior.

6

Sick or Sinful?

◆

This chapter is essential reading for anyone who is serious about overcoming anxiety, stress, and frustration. Let's first set the context by considering two passages from Proverbs:

> *Do not be wise in your own eyes; fear the LORD and shun evil. This will bring health to your body and nourishment to your bones (Proverbs 3:7,8).*
>
> *A man's spirit sustains him in sickness, but a crushed spirit who can bear? (Proverbs 18:14).*

One of our responsibilities as Christians is to be witnesses to weary travelers who are trying to use human resources to deal with sin. The collapse of family life and the escalation of dishonesty, stealing, violence, crime, physical abuse, and sexual abuse speaks for itself.

Our world needs a good dose of love, joy, peace, long-suffering, kindness, goodness, faithfulness, gentleness, and self-control.

Before I went to college I spent hour after hour studying the Bible. I came across words like anger, resentment, fear, bitterness, rebellion, murmuring, dishonesty, lust, jealousy, fornication, and stealing. They were called sins, or works of the flesh.

I would share this information with the restless, nervous people who crossed my path. Many of them could see that some of these sins were present in their lives. They repented of their sins and their restless, nervous symptoms disappeared.

This happened often enough that I decided to return to college to learn more about a biblical approach to human behavior.

In my sociology and psychology classes I learned that the same words the Bible uses to describe sin were used to describe personality or emotional disorders. In those days we frequently heard the term "nervous breakdown." People who had nervous breakdowns would be quickly hospitalized. The patient was "sick" and required a psychiatrist who could prescribe medication and use a specialized form of treatment called therapy. The patient was struggling with what was called a "neurosis" (an emotional disorder with physical complaints without objective evidence of disease).

A New View of Sin

Ten years later I hung out my first Christian counseling shingle. A letter sent to a group of pastors announcing my availability resulted in a full schedule within a few months.

A pattern emerged rather quickly. Many people were coming to find a cure for an anxiety state that was intolerable.

In the background these people would be struggling with a marriage problem, parent/child relations, difficulty socializing, or conflict at work. The responses to these problems were predictable: anger, resentment, fear, bitterness, rebellion, griping, yelling, dishonesty, lust, jealousy, sex, or stealing. The attempt to contain such emotions and desires caused these people to become highly excitable, unnaturally apprehensive, and very restless. Such a condition cannot be tolerated for long.

Curiously, these people had also acquired a new vocabulary. Ten years earlier it was not difficult for them to talk about sin and see their problems as such.

Now my counselees would leave my office greatly relieved only as long as we focused on their circumstances past and present. They wanted to focus on what caused their emotional reactions, and not deal with the emotional reactions themselves.

My teachers in graduate school taught that a personality disorder is not a person's own fault. The Freudian hypothesis was that neurosis stems from a too-severe handling at the hands of harsh, unloving parents and an irrational society. The individual has done nothing "sinful," but rather is forced to repress what he wants to do. Thus he is sick, not sinful—the innocent victim of "the demands of the fathers." Rogers, a leading psychologist at that time, insisted that we are inherently good and yet are corrupted by our experiences with the external everyday world.

These psychological explanations for personal unrest eventually filtered down to the churches of this nation, and now I was facing the incredible fact that dealing with sin was totally ruled out in the psychological world and was rapidly disappearing in the church as well.

The emphasis among Christians was slowly changed from dealing with sins to coming to terms with past experiences. These people expected sympathy and acceptance while others around them lovingly helped them to recover from their sicknesses.

Many of these counselees required many months of "therapy" in order to get control of themselves. They would be taught to become aware of the people or circumstances that triggered their negative emotions or behavior patterns. They learned to interrupt a line of conversation when they sensed they were becoming "disturbed" and to avoid certain people or circumstances. One man was told that when he felt his jaws tighten he must interrupt whomever he was talking to. He would change the subject, leave the room, walk around the block, or go for a ride.

I became a partner with these counselees. They could share their failures with me and I was there to give them a warm, sympathetic welcome. After months of therapy we were not far from where we started. *I guess therapy simply takes a long time,* I told myself. All went well as long as the counselee could set the pace and determine the content of our conversations.

All too frequently I encountered stiff resistance when I proposed that we take a look into the Bible to see what it had to say about emotions and behavior patterns. My dilemma was that my clients' emotional problems were often coupled with a headache or abdominal pain. I felt the pressure of trying to decide if they should be sent to see a physician. On the other hand, some contacted me at the recommendation of a physician.

Della, the woman we met in chapter 3, is an example of a person who was seeing a physician but came to see me on her own. Were these "nervous" people sick or sinful? Or both? I couldn't answer the first part. But if they were sinful, I could attempt to help them find out.

The Disappearance of Sin

In 1960, Dr. O. Hobart Mowrer, the president of the American Psychological Association, wrote a paper entitled, "Sin, the Lesser of Two Evils." He did not come to the same conclusions that I did, but he did help me clarify my thinking.

He related an incident that happened while teaching a summer session. A student said to him, "Did you know that near the beginning of the course you created a kind of scandal on this campus? You used the word 'sin' without saying 'so-called' or making a joke about it." This was virtually unheard of in a psychology professor and had occasioned considerable dismay and perplexity.

Read that last paragraph again! It's clear that non-Christians reject the concept of sin. But among Christians, doesn't the mass rejection of the concept of sin strike you as strange? Christians everywhere are turning to psychotherapy and medicine for help with their sins.

My experience with the concept of sin paralleled what Dr. Mowrer was describing both in and out of the church. When was the last time you had a discussion about sin? The word "sin," at the time of this writing, has all but disappeared.

I became a Christian because I understood that Jesus died to save us from our sins (Matthew 1:21) and I unquestionably needed to be saved from my sins. Isn't this the issue that separates Christianity from secular humanism? The Person of Christ died for our sins and was raised to life again so that we could be victorious over sin.

Let's look at Mowrer's concept of sin:

> Traditionally, sin has been thought of as whatever causes one to go to Hell; and since Hell, as a place of other worldly retribution and torment, has conveniently dropped out of most religious as well as secular thought, the concept of sin might indeed seem antiquated and absurd. But, as I observed in a Cincinnati paper, Hell is still very much with us in those states of mind and being which we call neurosis and psychosis; and I have come to increasingly, at least in my own mind, identify anything that carries us toward these forms of perdition as sin. Irresponsibility, wrongdoing, immorality, sin: what do the terms matter if we can thus understand more accurately the nature of psychopathology and gain greater practical control over its ramified forms and manifestations?[1]

Did you catch his emphasis? Anything that draws us toward neurosis or psychosis is sin. The "sickness" approach was not solving the patient's problem. The psychiatrist had not demonstrated that psychoanalysis, tranquilizers or various forms of chemotherapy were curative. Thus, Mowrer concluded that in regard to the concept of sin and that of sickness, sin is the lesser of two evils.

Mowrer described a most surprising difficulty that I was struggling with also. At the very time that psychologists were becoming distrustful of the sickness approach to personality disturbances and were beginning to look more favorably at moral and religious precepts, clergymen were getting caught up and bedazzled by the sickness approach. Ministers were departing from their position on the true sinful nature of human existence and the "living death" that results.

Alas, I have not seen any turnaround as of this writing.

Mowrer then asks, If we attribute emotional disorders to sin, then what should our attitude be toward the sinner? Nonjudgmental? Nondirective? Warm? Accepting? Ethically neutral?

The prevailing opinion these days is that we can get the sinner to love himself by loving him and accepting him. This flows from the Freudian assumption that the patient is not really guilty or sinful but only fancies himself so, and from Roger's view that we are inherently good and are corrupted by our experiences with the external, everyday world. Mowrer then raises what I believe is the critical issue:

> For the only way to resolve the paradox of self-hatred and self-punishment is to assume, not that it represents merely an "interjection" of the attitudes of others, but that the self-hatred is realistically justified and will persist until the individual, by radically altered attitude and action, honestly and realistically comes to feel that he now deserves something better. . . .
>
> Just so long as a person lives under the shadow of real, unacknowledged, and unexpiated guilt, he cannot (if he has any character at all) "accept himself"; and all our efforts to reassure and accept him will avail nothing. He will continue to hate himself and to suffer the inevitable consequences of self-hatred. . . .

As long as one remains, in old-fashioned religious phraseology, hard-of-heart and unrepentant, just so long will one's conscience hold him in the vise-like grip of "neurotic" rigidity and suffering. . . .

But the moment he (with or without "assistance") begins to accept his guilt and his sinfulness, the possibility of radical reformation opens up, and with this, the individual may legitimately, though not without pain and effort, pass from deep, pervasive self-rejection and self-torture to a new freedom, of self-respect and peace.[2]

Thus we arrive, says Mowrer, not only at a new (really, a very old) conception of the nature of "neurosis" which may change our entire approach to this problem, but also at an understanding of one of the most fundamental fallacies of Freudian psychoanalysis and many other kindred efforts at psychotherapy: that the person is not really sinful or guilty.

Freud observed, quite accurately, that the neurotic tortures himself; and he conjectured that this type of suffering arose from the irrationality and overseverity of the superego (the part of you that mediates your personal desires and those of the people around you).

But at once there was an empirical as well as logical difficulty which Freud (unlike some of his followers) faithfully acknowledged. In his *New Introductory Lectures and Psychoanalysis* (1933), which Mowrer quoted, he said:

If the parents have really ruled with a rod of iron, we easily understand the child developing a severe superego, but, contrary to our expectations, experience shows that the superego may reflect

the same relentless harshness even when the upbringing has been gentle and kind.[3]

And then Freud adds, candidly: "We ourselves do
not feel that we have fully understood it."[4]

This is an important point. He is saying that it's
possible for a patient to recall only the harshness and
severity of the parents and ignore the loving care he
received. Some patients reflect the same harshness even
when their upbringing was gentle and kind.

Mowrer agrees with Freud that the patient's suffering cannot be explained only because of harsh treatment
in the past. The neurotic tortures himself because of his
knowledge of himself. Mowrer then adds a pessimistic
note:

> But here we too, like Freud, encounter a diffi-
> culty. There is some evidence that human beings do
> not change radically unless they first acknowledge
> their sins; but we also know how hard it is for one
> to make such an acknowledgment unless he has
> already changed. In other words, the full realiza-
> tion of deep worthlessness is a severe ego "insult";
> and must have some new source of strength, it
> seems, to endure it. This is a mystery (or is it only a
> mistaken observation?) which traditional theology
> has tried to resolve in various ways—without com-
> plete success. Can we psychologists do better?[5]

7

The Missing Link

◆

In the close of the previous chapter, Mowrer concluded his article with a question: Can we psychologists do better? I presume he meant better than the medical doctor or the minister.

Looking back 50 years, we can evaluate the combined efforts of the medical, social, educational, governmental, legal, and theological professions. The combined impact on society has been negative. There are exceptions here and there, but in general, human misery has worsened.

The Need for Repentance and Forgiveness

In the early sixties, I listened to many counselees tell me their troubles. Most of them chose not to seek forgiveness of sins. They chose to live with their sins.

I had to make a choice. Go with the flow, or go with the few who would seek repentance and forgiveness of their sins.

After a little reflection, I made the decision that I would make the diagnosis of sin my primary goal in helping people. Sin (resentment, anger, hatred, rebellion) had nearly destroyed my own life and marriage. If I understood my Bible correctly, the "emotional" problems that plagued my counselees were sin. A brief review of some of the Bible verses that had guided me in those early days were refreshing to my spirit:

> *He who conceals his sins does not prosper, but whoever confesses and renounces them finds mercy (Proverbs 28:13).*

> *Your iniquities have separated you from your God; your sins have hidden his face from you, so that he will not hear (Isaiah 59:2).*

> *When he comes, he will convict the world of guilt in regard to sin and righteousness and judgment (John 16:8).*

> *Look, the Lamb of God, who takes away the sin of the world! (John 1:29).*

> *Blessed is he whose transgressions are forgiven, whose sins are covered (Psalm 32:1).*

The bad news is, there is no human remedy for sin.

The good news is, repentance for sin before God brings instant cleansing.

The sad news is, the word "sin" has nearly disappeared.

Dr. Mowrer gave a precise description of the struggle that I see people going through: "the full realization of deep worthlessness is a severe ego 'insult'; and must have some new source of strength...to endure it."[1] Mowrer's article leaves me with two observations:

1. He offers no basis for defining sin.

2. He offers no source of strength to endure the process.

Mowrer is not referring to sin as a violation of God's laws. In his scenario, God is not in the picture. Rather, he is referring to the individual in relation to other human beings. He says that the suffering person must acknowledge his own guilt, forgive himself, and make restitution if necessary.

Defining Sin and Its Cure

After He arose from the dead and was ready to ascend into heaven, Jesus gave His disciples one last word, quoting from the Scriptures in reference to Himself: "Repentance and forgiveness of sins will be preached in His name to all nations" (Luke 24:47).

"In His name" is the missing link.

The Bible offers help for both a definition of sin and a source of strength to repent and be forgiven of sin. The chart on pages 96-97 gives a partial word-picture of sin and the benefits of walking in the Spirit. This information is based on Mark 7:21-23, Romans 1:28-31, Galatians 5:19-21, Ephesians 4:25-31, and 2 Timothy 3:1-5.

What must we know to *take* the necessary steps toward spirit-controlled living?

Spirit-Controlled Living versus Sin-Controlled Living

Spirit-Filled Mind		Sins of the Mind	
forgiveness	humility	unforgiveness	pride
hope	thankfulness	evil thoughts	ingratitude
appreciation	confidence	covetousness	selfish ambition
willingness	wisdom	greed	deceitfulness
impartiality		lust	

Spirit-Filled Emotions		Sinful Emotions	
love	joy	hatred	anger
peace	long-suffering	rebellion	unloving attitude
gentle spirit	kind spirit	bitterness	jealousy
gladness		envy	malice
		bad temper	

Spirit-Controlled Living versus Sin-Controlled Living cont.

Spirit-Filled Mouth		Sins of the Mouth	
truthfulness	praise	lying	slandering
thankfulness	timeliness	complaining	disputing
gentle answer	soothing tongue	yelling	backbiting
encouraging	pleasant words	contentiousness	quarrelsomeness
tact		boasting	blasphemy

Spirit-Filled Behavior		Sinful Behavior	
kindness	gentleness	fornication	brutality
righteousness	self-control	adultery	without self-control
obedience	cooperation	drunkenness	stealing
goodness	sincerity	murder	violence
courage	willing to serve	revelry	disobedience

It Takes Faith to Approach God

Hebrews 11:6 tells us, "Without faith it is impossible to please God, because anyone who comes to him must believe that he exists and that he rewards those who earnestly seek him."

Whether or not there is a God is doubtable, just as it is doubtable if a plane in flight will land safely. People take a step of faith every time they board a plane. To call on God also requires a step of faith.

By faith, the humanist believes that God does not exist.

By faith, Carl Rogers believed that we are inherently good and are corrupted by our experiences with the external, everyday world.

By faith, Freud made the assumption that we are not really sinful or guilty but only fancy ourselves so.

By faith, we Christians believe that God exists, that Jesus is the Son of God, and that through Him we receive forgiveness and cleansing for our sins.

By faith, we believe that the Holy Spirit empowers us to walk in the Spirit.

By faith, most Christians believe what Jesus said to His Father when He prayed, "Your word is truth" (John 17:17).

Jesus said to a crowd of people, "Blessed rather are those who hear the word of God and obey it" (Luke 11:28). The apostle Paul wrote, "Through the law we become conscious of sin" (Romans 3:20).

By faith, those of us who accept the Word of God (the Bible) as truth will measure what we read or hear by the Bible. The Bible states, "Do your best to present yourself to God as one approved, a workman who does not need to be ashamed and who correctly handles the word of truth" (2 Timothy 2:15).

Sin Has Separated Man from God

Romans 3:23 says, "For all have sinned and fall short of the glory of God." And Romans 3:10 states plainly, "There is no one righteous, not even one."

Since this is true, trouble exposes the basically sinful and unrighteous nature of a man. This raises an important question: "What is sin and unrighteousness?" We turn to the Bible for the answer: "Everyone who commits sin breaks God's law, for that is what sin is, by definition—a breaking of God's law" (1 John 3:4 PHILLIPS).

A sinner has transgressed the law of God in the same sense that a traffic violator has transgressed a traffic law. Nothing can change the fact that he is a *violator*. We have all experienced the sense of relief that comes after traveling through a 20-mile-per-hour traffic zone at 40 miles per hour. We vaguely experience the same tension when we violate any law of God. Thus, *sinner* and *violator* are alike in meaning.

While a young Christian, praying often seemed like little more than talking to myself. Then I stumbled across a very meaningful Bible verse:

> Surely the arm of the LORD is not too short to save, nor his ear too dull to hear. But your iniquities have separated you from your God; your sins have hidden his face from you, so that he will not hear (Isaiah 59:1,2).

To declare that man has sinned—that is, to say he is out of line with God's standard—is not to condemn him. The Bible gives us the key to freedom from the severe ego insult (condemnation) that is the result of seeing one's sinfulness.

There is no human remedy for sin. Yet sin is the

simplest problem in the world to solve. The resources of God, the Creator of the universe, are available to anyone who asks—on God's terms.

You Approach God Through
His Son Jesus Christ

A variety of Bible verses give some guidance:

> *For God did not send his Son into the world to condemn the world, but to save the world through him. Whoever believes in him is not condemned, but whoever does not believe stands condemned already because he has not believed in the name of God's one and only Son (John 3:17,18).*

> *Jesus answered, "I am the way and the truth and the life. No one comes to the Father except through me" (John 14:6).*

> *Salvation is found in no one else, for there is no other name under heaven given to men by which we must be saved (Acts 4:12).*

Anyone who is knowledgeable in the mass of secular writing about the nature of the human being understands that to accept the above three verses and the ones that follow requires a major step of faith.

Confession of Your Sin and God's Forgiveness
Brings Cleansing and Healing

Mowrer is right; acknowledging one's sins is a severe ego insult. Jesus gave the reason:

> *This is the verdict: Light has come into the world, but men loved darkness instead of light*

because their deeds were evil. Everyone who does evil
hates the light, and will not come into the light for
fear that his deeds will be exposed (John 3:19,20).

God's offer is still available: "If we confess our sins,
he is faithful and just and will forgive us our sins and
purify us from all unrighteousness" (1 John 1:9).

True repentance leaves one relieved (well) because
God has forgiven, cleansed, and renewed. Yet repentance is rare. I seldom see true repentance. Following
renewal, it's possible that some restitution may need to
be made. This would be the result of renewal, not a
condition for renewal.

As I write this sentence, I am looking out at the
Atlantic Ocean. The sun is just now rising out of the east
in a blaze of colorful splendor—reminding me of a biblical promise: "As far as the east is from the west, so far has
he removed our transgressions from us" (Psalm 103:12).

Our World Needs Spirit-Controlled People

Our world needs love, joy, peace, long-suffering,
kindness, goodness, faithfulness, gentleness, and self-
control; it needs a good dose of these virtues.

Most mental-health workers would agree with that
statement. We would, however, sharply disagree on
how to generate such virtues. If you were an atheist,
your only option would be to find a way to create an
environment that will either produce these qualities
inside a person or release them from within a person,
assuming something is blocking their release.

I spoke with a man who wished that he had love,
joy, and peace in his home. While the man had great
wealth, he realized that he could not find a doctor, counselor, or a retail store where he could buy love, joy, and

peace. He admitted that everything he had tried in this world—money, fame, and power—had not brought happiness. These virtues are not available "over the counter." Qualities such as love, joy, and peace are only available as a result of a relationship with Jesus Christ. It is a shame that many people in our world today will not accept this fact.

God Is the Source

The Bible says these virtues are from a source out of this world. God controls an infinite supply. They will flow through the person who is cleansed from sin as his body is yielded to the Spirit of God. The result is access to a supernatural resource that a person can draw upon.

Drawing upon God can be compared to drawing water. When you open a faucet, water flows out. Water is made up of two parts: hydrogen, a gas; and oxygen, also a gas. These invisible units combine miraculously into a product called water. A glassful will quench your thirst. You can fill a tub and take a bath in it. You can irrigate a thousand-acre farm with it.

You can use all you want because you are drawing from a reservoir of water. All you need to do is to keep the pipes in good repair, and open the faucet. The water will flow. Amazingly, you can stop the flow of a massive reservoir of water by simply closing the faucet.

In similar fashion, when you allow Jesus to come into your body as your Savior, not only are you cleansed from your sin, but you also have access to the Spirit of God. Here is an invisible, unexplainable presence that produces visible, measurable changes in the way your body works. Your body is transformed.

Phillip Keller describes this miracle:

... deceivers become honest; the vile become noble; the vicious become gentle; the selfish become selfless; the hard-hearted become affectionate; the weak become strong. Once a person is yielded to the Holy Spirit, there can be no pretending to be pleasant and pious while within one seethes and boils with pent-up perversions. Apart from the Spirit of God in control, other human beings' ill will, hatred, bitterness, envy, old grudges, jealousy and other heinous attitudes can be masked with a casual shrug or forced half smile.[2]

Nothing in *this world* can cause a person to change so radically. No longer do circumstances or people determine the condition under your skin. You can now respond to the troublesome people in your life with unconditional love, joy, peace, long-suffering, kindness, goodness, faithfulness, gentleness, and self-control. Humanly speaking, this is an impossibility. But, by yielding yourself to the Spirit of God, an infinite, endless supply flows through you. There is enough for a minor irritation or a major tragedy.

I watched the life of my wife of 42 years slowly ebb away, discovered that I had Parkinson's disease, and experienced a business loss of more than $250,000 all at the same time. There was enough peace, joy, and comfort to draw upon for each day while all three events were happening. Yet the will to draw upon the supply must come from me. No other human being or event can stop this from happening in me. However, I can, by an act of my will, cease to yield and stop the flow of this infinite supply in my body.

However, as long as I yield my body to the Spirit of God, day by day, there is an infinite supply for all of life's irritations and tragedies.

I want to share a letter with you that gives us hope in approaching God by faith:

It was January '68, I had a terrible bout with colitis again. The doctor had told me I would never be free of it totally—I'd have to watch my diet and stay on the medication indefinitely. Inside I was panicking, "knew" it would soon be the end and my three children would be orphans. My husband pastored a small congregation and a new member encouraged us to go to a CCC [Campus Crusade for Christ] conference at Lake Yale that spring. She had no idea about the tormenting turmoil within me. Somehow I was able to function outwardly so that no one knew what was going on inwardly. All my life I had lived with fear. There were periods of reprieve but like a hidden monster fear would come again stronger and more devastating than before.

At age 8, polio became rampant and I "knew" I would have to spend the rest of my life in an iron lung. Then there were the missionary films of leper colonies. I would look for white spots on my skin and at times I would take pins and prick the spots to be sure I still had feeling in them.

At the age of 14 I was chewing gum and accidentally bit the inside of my cheek; it turned sort of a whitish color and I was again in a panic. I asked the Lord to heal it and if He would I would never put another stick of gum in my mouth. On and on they came—unreasonable fears in different disguises, yet always the same gnawing. They were so illogical yet I couldn't shake them. Tenaciously they held on against all my arguments and reasoning. I was too ashamed to admit to anyone the torment I felt so deep inside.

I had fallen in love and our wedding was planned. Now it was breast cancer—my girlfriend's mother had recently died and I was so sure I would marry and become a burden and a heartache to my young husband and I just couldn't do that so for the first time in my life I admitted to someone, my doctor, that I had fears (not of my fear history, but of my present fear). He assured me I was perfectly healthy, but under a lot of pressure and gave me my first tranquilizer.

I was elated—I was thrilled—there was nothing wrong with me! I could marry and live happily ever after. My freedom didn't last long.

While my husband attended Bob Jones University I gave birth to three children. I would wake up in a cold sweat, shaking in the bed unable to get my breath begging my husband to pray for me. The doctors continued to tell me that I was just under pressure: three children, husband in college, and having to make ends meet was too much for any girl and since we couldn't afford a vacation—one in a bottle (tranquilizers) was next best.

After graduation we returned to Florida and started a nondenominational church. It was at this time we decided to attend the Lay Institute for Evangelism at Lake Yale. I had gone for a pap test but had not gone for the results knowing that it would be positive and our vacation at Lake Yale would be spoiled. I would wait until we came back to get the results.

I knew after listening to Dr. Brandt's morning devotional that I had to talk with him. Somehow I knew that the Lord could help me through this man, but I was too frightened to get an appointment. I told my husband to please push me, but all his coaxing didn't help. The last day of the conference he finally went and made the appointment himself. We sat across from him and I was paralyzed with fear. The words refused to come. Dr. Brandt waited patiently for an answer to his question, "What's the problem?" Finally my husband broke the silence and told him of my unreasonable fears. After a moment Dr. Brandt looked me square in the eyes and said, "Who do you hate?" Me? I was insulted and proceeded to explain to this man that I was a loving, wonderful Christian and I didn't hate anyone—I loved everyone. I was a very self-sacrificing person. If I had thought he had the answer this certainly wasn't it. He shared how perfect love casts out fear. God has not given us a spirit of fear but of love and of power and of a sound mind. He politely but firmly let me know I did not have a sound mind. I had no perfected love or fear would have left. I felt that could be right, but surely not that hate part. Again I tried to enlighten him. These fears had been there even when I was a child. But he would not be enlightened. Looking me straight in the eye again, his only comment was, "Who did you hate as a child?" I just couldn't accept this, but God knew I wanted to be free. I agreed by an act of my will to receive what he was saying as truth, but what was I to do with this information? If it was true that I hated someone, I certainly didn't know who it could possibly be. I was a very forgiving person (I had forgotten the Scripture that tells us how the heart is deceitful above all things and desperately wicked). His simple counsel was to go off by myself and ask God to show me who in fact did I hate. I must forgive them. I must ask the Lord for forgiveness for my unforgiveness.

Sitting in the car under a beautiful oak covered with Spanish moss God spoke clearly and unmistakably to me. My young life came before me like a ticker tape: My Dad, my Grandmother, stepfathers and many others whom I still held IOUs against. A Godly repentance I had never experienced in my life swept over me. From my innermost being I cried to my God and He delivered me. I don't know how long we embraced, Jesus and me, but I knew I was cleansed and I knew I was free.

I ran to our cabin, grabbed my husband's hand and announced we were going to the snack shop. As we walked hand in hand we both knew intuitively what we were going to buy. Yes, Hallelujah. A pack of Wrigley's Spearmint gum and I put all 5 pieces in my mouth. It had been a full 14 years since a stick of gum had been in my mouth. I was free! Free, even to chew gum again or not to chew, but I was free.

Twenty-four years later, I'm still free. I have never been tormented again, for he whom the Son has made free is free indeed. AMEN!

Repentant people are free—cleansed, renewed, restored. Repentance restores your reason (conscience) and fellowship (with the Lord). Restoration brings wholeness to your being and to your relationships with others.

Possessing the Right Perspective

Sick, or sinful? When Eva was ill with a fatal cancer, she learned a lesson and taught it to me. You can be sick *and* sinful. She cautioned us not to jump to the conclusion that emotional reactions while you are sick are caused by being sick.

One example will suffice. When she told me this story, she was enduring a lot of pain. But her eyes sparkled and she seemed pleased as though she had received a pearl of great price.

Eva's pride and joy was her kitchen. But there came a stage in her illness when she was bedridden and could no longer work in the kitchen. Many friends came to help. She could hear them in her kitchen. She would nurse waves of anger and resentment because she couldn't control her kitchen. It didn't matter that she never verbalized her feelings; her attitude was unacceptable in God's presence.

She is not sure how it happened. As she lay there it became crystal clear to her that she was nursing a sinful heart. It was as though someone offered to clean it up by removing the bad attitudes and replacing them with gratitude and joy. She thinks it was the Lord. She had a choice: She could keep her sinful heart, or choose cleansing and joy. She chose the latter.

Her last month on this earth was a time when she was so appreciative and content it seemed unreal. It was!

I am mystified that anyone would turn his back on the invitation to find rest because he refuses to take a step of faith. God's Word gives a perfect solution: "A heart at peace gives life to the body, but envy rots the bones" (Proverbs 14:30).

> *God had one son on earth without sin, but never one without suffering*—Saint Augustine.[3]

8

How to Deal with Your Anger

◆

The *American Heritage Dictionary* defines anger this way:

an•ger (áng′g•r)—n. 1. A feeling of extreme displeasure, hostility, indignation, or exasperation toward someone or something; rage; wrath; ire. 2. OBSOLETE. Trouble; pain; affliction.

SYNONYMS: ANGER, RAGE, FURY, IRE, WRATH, RESENTMENT, INDIGNATION.

These nouns denote varying degrees of marked displeasure. Anger, the most general, denotes strong, usually temporary displeasure without specifying manner of expression. Rage and fury are closely related in the sense of intense, uncontained, explosive emotion. Fury can be more destructive, rage more justified by circumstances. Ire is a poetic term for anger. Wrath applies especially to fervid anger that seeks vengeance or punishment on an epic scale. Resentment refers to ill will and suppressed anger generated by a sense of grievance. One feels indignation at seeing the mistreatment of someone or something dear and worthy.[1]

The Universality of Anger

Not everyone is an alcoholic; not everyone steals, or swears, or commits adultery. But as far as I know, *everyone struggles with anger*. It is a universal problem. I have observed it among primitive cannibals in Irian Jaya, among uncivilized Indians in the remote jungles of Brazil, among illiterate people in tiny villages deep in the forest of Zaire, among my playmates when I was a child, in my parents, in church members, in pastors, in highly educated people, in the very rich, in people in government, and yes, in me.

You cannot decide to be angry. You can take elaborate precautions to avoid being angry. But, alas, sooner or later anger underneath your skin is triggered by a memory, someone's behavior, a conversation, a phone call, or a letter. It can cause your heart to beat faster, make you sweat, tense up your muscles, foul up your digestive system, alter the way you think, dictate how you act, and trigger negative words from your mouth.

There seems to be universal agreement that anger must be tamed. Yet there is vast disagreement over the cause and the cure.

I have been aware of anger within me as far back as I can remember and up to this very day. Usually I could ignore it, express it safely to close people like my parents, swallow it, or work it off in various activities like tennis or basketball.

The first time that I was conscious that I could not manage my anger occurred in my late twenties. At that time, I had a boss who kept me riled up most of the day, a wife who persisted in frustrating me by doing things her way rather than my way, and a tiny toddler who irritated me constantly by simply wanting my attention when I didn't want to give it. These three people backed me into a corner. They didn't even know it. They forced me to face up to the fact that there was something in me that was activated by them and turned me into a person who said things I was sorry for, did things that I regretted, thought things that frightened me, and caused my body (heart, stomach, and muscles) to malfunction.

The solution came for me when I was convinced that I was helpless and needed to be saved from myself. The Bible described my condition exactly: "Now if I do what I do not want to do, it is no longer I who do it, but it is sin living in me that does it" (Romans 7:20). There was no quibbling about whom that verse applied to; it described me perfectly. This was clearly the law of sin controlling my body.

A Faulty Perception of Anger

This sentence sums up what almost everyone says when they come to the consulting room with an anger problem: "My anger is a normal and justifiable response to the way I was treated."

No one inquires about the possibility of anger being a sin in their hearts. That word has almost disappeared from their vocabulary. They seek relief from restlessness, nervousness, anxiety. The buzzwords are "stressed out" or "burned out." They are disturbed about their relationships to a narrow world of partners, children, other family members, social contacts, and people at work or church. People admit anger reluctantly. If they do admit it, they are quick to justify it.

Individuals do come to seek advice when they are the recipient of someone else's anger. For example, a wife will talk to me about her husband: "When in a good mood, Ted is a pleasant person to be around, but if you catch him when he's mad—look out.

"I can tell his mood by the way he shuts the door," his wife says. "If he nearly breaks the window in slamming it, I brace myself for his first gripe."

And come it will, followed by other complaints. "Why don't you make those kids keep their bicycles out of the driveway?" "Turn off that TV. There's racket enough around here without that thing adding to it!" "Women drivers! They should be kept off the highways after 3:00 in the afternoon!"

Anger Is Destructive Energy

Negative responses such as these can cause much misery in life. Edward Strecker and Kenneth Appel have compiled a list of words that people use to describe anger:

> When the presence of anger is detected in a person we say he is mad, bitter, frustrated, griped, fed up, sore, hot under the collar, excited (now don't get excited), seething, annoyed, troubled, inflamed, indignant, antagonistic, exasperated, vexed, furious, provoked, hurt, irked, sick (she makes me sick), pained (he gives me a pain), cross, hostile, ferocious, savage, vicious, deadly, dangerous, offensive.

Then, since anger is energy and impels individuals to do things intending to hurt or destroy, there is a whole series of verbs which depict actions motivated by anger: to hate, wound, damage, annihilate, despise, scorn, disdain, loathe, vilify, curse, despoil, ruin, demolish, abhor, abominate, desolate, ridicule, tease, kid, get even, laugh at, humiliate, goad, shame, criticize, cut, take out spite on, rail at, scold, bawl out, humble, irritate, beat up, take for a ride, ostracize, fight, beat, vanquish, compete with, brutalize, curse, offend, bully.[2]

It is my observation that almost everyone resists calling any kind of anger sin. Multitudes of people (including me) have faced up to problems such as drinking, swearing, or stealing as sin and now it's behind us. It's been dealt with.

Dealing with anger is different. You can be completely and totally repentant over your anger. Confession leads to welcome relief from tension. I suspect that most people (me, too) experience some anger every week. You think you have dealt with it, and it shows up again.

I have observed that one difficulty in dealing with anger is the wide range of intensity with which it can be expressed. On the one end there is such extreme anger that it leads to violent physical abuse or even murder. We have no difficulty recognizing such anger as sin. But on the other end of the continuum is anger that is so mild as to be almost unnoticeable. This "annoyance level" of anger is easy to ignore; for example, mild frustration at a child who won't make his bed, at a nearly empty gas tank in the car, at a traffic light, or at an impolite clerk.

You can compare anger to the flow of contaminated water into a tub. A wide-open faucet yields the same kind of water as a dripping faucet. One drop at a time will gradually fill a tub if the drain hole is plugged. It may take weeks to fill the tub with contaminated water, but eventually there will come a time when one more drop will make the water spill over the top. All that water came from the same polluted source.

Extreme anger is easy to recognize and impossible to ignore. The body pumps adrenaline into the bloodstream, causing the heartbeat to accelerate, the blood pressure to rise, the mouth to become dry, the muscles to become tense, the mental faculties to become alert, and the emotions to become disturbed.

A drop of anger is not as easy to recognize. To put it another way, it is easy to ignore. Bodily changes are hardly noticeable, but the effects are cumulative. The symptoms are anxiety, restlessness, tension. Drops of anger build up in the body. Eventually, one more incident (major or minor), and anger spills over the top. I listen to people who are puzzled over certain responses that surprise themselves:

> "I heard myself screaming at the children to come into the house."

> "I was so mad I actually hit her. It was over which tie I should wear."

> "He lives a thousand miles away. At times when someone mentions his name I am fully consumed with anger in a matter of seconds."

Anger Can Build Up Slowly

Wayne Hartley was an angry man. He moved from job to job because "worldly people" irked him. Finally he landed a job at a firm with a Christian president. Here was a man he felt he could work for; he looked forward to a happy relationship on the job.

But things did not turn out that way. Hartley was made a general manager and had a number of foremen to supervise. One of the foremen used a great deal of profanity. One day Hartley could stand his talk no longer, so he called him aside and ordered him to refrain. The foreman paid no attention, so Hartley warned him again, "Stop it, or you'll get fired!"

The company president heard about Hartley's ultimatum. He called in his general manager. "Joe has a foul mouth, I know," the president said. "But he gets more work out of his crew than any of our other foremen."

He told Hartley to leave the man alone. Hartley was not to impose his private standards on Joe or any other employee. Reluctantly Hartley accepted the president's directive. But from that day on he felt he was constantly being overruled by the president. One day when he heard the foreman curse, it was the drop that spilled over the top. He stormed into the president's office, demanding a showdown.

"Am I the general manager or not?" he thundered.

"Why do you ask? Do you think you are the president?"

Wayne Hartley saw red. He shouted at his superior, waving his finger under his boss's nose. He was completely angry—from the top of his head to the bottom of his feet. That reminds me of George Jean Nathan's saying, "No man can think clearly when his fists are clenched."[3]

Telling of the incident later, Hartley said, "It takes a lot to get me mad, but when I am, the fur really flies. There we stood, toe-to-toe and nose-to-nose, yelling at each other. And both of us professed to be Christians. But you can be sure of this: No non-Christian ever made me more miserable than that man."

Did the company president cause Wayne Hartley to blow up?

"Who else?" Wayne demanded. "The last time he crossed me was the very last straw. I don't lose control of myself unless I'm forced to."

In looking back over his life, Wayne Hartley could see that he had possessed an antagonistic spirit since childhood. It had come out at home, at school, toward his wife, toward his children, toward anyone who thwarted him. He did not blow up very often, but when he did, everyone got out of his way. He controlled things pretty well by simply threatening to blow up. At times, however, he met people who just let him blow. This was true of the people he worked with; and this explained why he moved from job to job. By such moves he was able to dismiss his own problem, saying that his reasons for moving were the worldliness, selfishness, or cantankerousness of others. He always had a good reason for his tantrums.

What was Wayne Hartley doing? He was accumulating wrath day after day. And he denied that he himself had anything to do with it.

His situation could be likened to the tub with a dripping faucet. Put the plug in and the tub fills up. The next drop will cause the water to run over. Is it the last drop that spills the water onto the floor? No, it's the last drop plus all the rest of the drops.

Wayne Hartley had an irritable attitude toward life. Tiny irritations at home, at church, at work, and on the way to and from work all slowly accumulated. At the same time, pressure was increasing. Usually he could work off some of the pressure and drain away some of the irritation. But occasionally he was trapped; the last drop, or "the last straw," would cause him to blow up.

Changing from Anger to Love

Conversations can sometimes take unexpected directions.

A calm, quiet-appearing man asked me some questions about his prayer life. But why would he seek me out rather than a minister? I discovered the answer after he answered a few questions.

He said, "I make promises to the Lord and ask Him for the help to carry them out, but I always fail. Then I feel let down by God, and that makes me feel guilty."

"What have you asked God to help you do?" I asked.

"I promised the Lord that I would get up at 5:30 every morning and spend an hour in devotions; but I am so sleepy I can't concentrate," he answered.

"Why do you want to get up at 5:30 A.M. for devotions?"

This question triggered the reason he came to see me. He had a "quick temper." I discovered that a casual conversation with his wife, which didn't go his way, could suddenly turn him into an angry, shouting person who would say mean, cutting words (not worth repeating).

He would punish his children severely over simple mistakes. In one instance, when one of his children reached across the table for a piece of bread instead of asking someone to pass it to her, in a flash of anger he hit her so hard that he knocked her off the chair. Another time he caught his son in the garage, a place known as off-limits to the children. The father hit his son so hard that he left a bruise.

And several months ago he was hospitalized for a few days for "nerves."

Thus, he thought it would help if he got up at 5:30 in the morning for devotions. This man was trying to do penance for his anger.

What the Bible Says About Anger

What biblical advice is there about the management of anger? Take a look:

> *Man's anger does not bring about the righteous life that God desires (James 1:20).*
>
> *Do not take revenge, my friends, but leave room for God's wrath, for it is written: "It is mine to avenge; I will repay," says the Lord (Romans 12:19).*
>
> *Get rid of all bitterness, rage and anger, brawling and slander, along with every form of malice (Ephesians 4:31).*

It seems clear to me that the Bible is telling us that God expects us to tackle the problems around us with His love in our hearts. Read on:

> *But I tell you: Love your enemies and pray for those who persecute you (Matthew 5:44).*
>
> *Husbands, love your wives (Ephesians 5:25).*
>
> *Wives, love your husbands (Titus 2:4).*
>
> *Mothers and fathers, love your children (Titus 2:4, Ephesians 6:4).*

Love your neighbor (Matthew 22:39).

Love the brotherhood of believers (1 Peter 2:17).

May the Lord make your love increase and overflow for each other and for everyone else (1 Thessalonians 3:12).

And hope does not disappoint us, because God has poured out his love into our hearts by the Holy Spirit, whom he has given us (Romans 5:5).

Who shall separate us from the love of Christ? Shall trouble or hardship or persecution or famine or nakedness or danger or sword? ... For I am convinced that neither death nor life, neither angels nor demons, neither the present nor the future, nor any powers, neither height nor depth, nor anything else in all creation, will be able to separate us from the love of God that is in Christ Jesus our Lord (Romans 8:35,38,39).

Jesus' response to evildoers, as they crucified Him between two criminals, was, "Father, forgive them, for they do not know what they are doing" (Luke 23:34).

But the difficult problem is, how can a human being, who naturally responds angrily to the circumstances of life, change from responding in anger to responding in love? Humanly speaking, we must admit that this biblical advice is impossible to attain. We all know that to bottle up or swallow anger is not the solution. Bottled-up anger can ruin your health and twist your thinking. You would become like a walking time bomb, set to explode at some eventual external provocation.

The Bible offers a radical solution: "Put it away. Stop it." This is humanly impossible. Yes, it takes a miracle. You need supernatural help.

The Steps to Change

Step 1:
Recognize Anger As Sin

The biblical prescription for dealing with destructive anger is precise and strong. Strife, malice, hatred, outbursts of wrath, dissension, contention, and the like are works of the flesh—of the sinful nature (Galatians 5:19-21, Colossians 3:8). They are sin, and that's good news because there is a divine solution for sin. God promised to help you. Dealing with sin is His specialty. Acts 4:12 says, "Salvation is found in no one else, for there is no other name under heaven given to men by which we must be saved."

A simple step that gives you a source of strength to "stop" angry responses is to invite Jesus to come into your life. Yet many competent, able people have a hard time accepting the fact that we need supernatural help.

"I can manage my anger. Isn't that good enough?" It certainly beats exploding. But the best you can do is to manage your anger. Only God can help you to "stop" because anger is sin. Therefore, you need a Savior who will cleanse you of your sins.

It is not inevitable that we must spend the rest of our lives struggling with anger. It can be "put away." Once we accept the fact that anger is sin and we need a Savior, we can practice a simple biblical directive—daily, if necessary: "If we confess our sins, he is faithful and just and will forgive us our sins and purify us from all unrighteousness" (1 John 1:9).

God will cleanse the anger out of our hearts. Anger is not good. It is bad; it is sin. It is destructive.

Step 2:
Replace Anger with Godly Emotions

When you have a forgiven, cleansed heart, you can ask God for the power of the Holy Spirit to produce the fruit of the Spirit in your life (Galatians 5:22,23):

love	goodness
joy	faithfulness
peace	gentleness
patience	self-control
kindness	

You will still have problems, face injustices, and encounter difficult people—as everyone does. You will still need to be energized, alerted, and motivated to correct what needs correcting. But a Christian knows that a person energized by the Holy Spirit with love, joy, peace, patience, kindness, goodness, faithfulness, gentleness, and self-control has the strength to conquer the bitter, sarcastic words; anxiety; bodily tensions; and violent behavior that formerly characterized him.

The apostle Paul says it best: "So I say, live by the Spirit, and you will not gratify the desires of the sinful nature" (Galatians 5:16).

A Christian does not always surrender to God perfectly any more than he can manage himself perfectly. Few people make it through any given day perfectly. But with God's help, you can catch anger at the earliest possible point.

An elated, middle-aged gentleman told me this story; I'll call him Mike:

He had made a poor decision that cost his company thousands of dollars. His boss called him and severely berated him over the phone. A contrite man hung up the phone and it rang again. It was his boss's boss, who proceeded to berate him also.

Mike felt himself becoming angry. Without interrupting the conversation, he repented and prayed for a peaceful heart. Before the conversation ended, he was fully relaxed.

When you realize you have sinned, take it to God. The apostle John says it well:

> *My dear children, I write this to you so that you will not sin. But if anybody does sin, we have one who speaks to the Father in our defense—Jesus Christ, the Righteous One. He is the atoning sacrifice for our sins, and not only for ours but also for the sins of the whole world (1 John 2:1,2).*

Ponder these verses:

> *First clean the inside of the cup and dish, and then the outside also will be clean (Matthew 23:26).*

> *God is spirit, and his worshipers must worship in spirit and in truth (John 4:24).*

> *So I say, live by the Spirit, and you will not gratify the desires of the sinful nature (Galatians 5:16).*

> *But the wisdom that comes from heaven is first of all pure; then peace loving, considerate, submissive, full of mercy and good fruit, impartial and sincere (James 3:17).*

> *And hope does not disappoint us, because God has poured out his love into our hearts by the Holy Spirit, whom he has given us (Romans 5:5).*

> *Man's anger does not bring about the righteous*
> *life that God desires (James 1:20).*

In this chapter, you'll notice there is a common thread running through the lives of the people who were struggling with their anger.

In my case, my boss, my wife, and my child triggered my anger. Eventually I simply took by faith that what these people triggered in me was sin. I needed to admit my sin and look to Jesus to cleanse me and give me a spirit of love. I grasped these biblical principles and found myself calming down without any of those three people changing one bit. A miracle!

The husband who came home, slammed the door, bawled out the children, and gave out some stupid orders was venting wrath that had accumulated over a series of little incidents that took place in his life. Though he might not be able to change his circumstances, he could have taken steps to change himself.

Our response to people and circumstances on the outside of us constantly reminds us of the condition inside us: an imperfect spiritual life which seems easier to justify or deny than to face.

Anger Reminds Us of Our Helplessness

We have the need for daily renewal of our lifetime dependency upon God. No one is exempt. There is none righteous. There is no human remedy. Daily dependence on God for help does not gradually change to self-sufficient independence. You should deal with anger as sin just as soon as you are aware of it, regardless of how mild your response is. Confession and repentance pull the plug and cleanse the heart of any anger lurking there. Do it as often as necessary.

Second Corinthians 9:8 shares these wonderful words: "God is able to make all grace abound to you, so that in all things at all times, having all that you need, you will abound in every good work."

Could such grace be available to Wayne Hartley? Yes. First, however, he had to take an honest look at himself. When he did, he saw that he brought a spirit of antagonism to his new job. He didn't like to be crossed—whether by the foreman who violated his standard of speech or by the president who refused to let Wayne impose his standard on another. The frustration of not getting his own way exposed the wrath within him.

For a long time he could not admit that he was an angry man. Therefore he had no need, no occasion to pray for forgiveness or grace. He needed none, he told himself.

"I get along fine unless someone else is unreasonable," he said. "And is it my fault if someone else is unreasonable?" Yet the Bible says, "Do not let the sun go down on *your* wrath" (Ephesians 4:26 NKJV, emphasis added).

When Wayne Hartley accepted the fact that the foreman's cursing triggered the wrath that was already in him, he could see that it was sin. You don't deal with your own sin by ordering someone else to stop cursing. You must go to God. He will cleanse you of your sin if you reach out for His help. He will give you a tender, compassionate heart toward the poor man who finds a crumb of relief by cursing.

And that is the good news for everyone who is filled with anger and malice and bitterness. The people in your life may never change their ways. Circumstances may be beyond your control. But fortunately you can do something about yourself. You can open your heart to God, who is able to fill it with bountiful grace. But whether you allow God to give you His grace is your decision.

Is Anger Always Wrong?

Strangely, most people who seek counsel will argue that they have the right to be angry. "Under my circumstances, can you blame me?" they will say in stout defense. Of course they have the right to be angry. But as long as they argue in defense of their wrath, they will see no need nor have any desire to change and thus be delivered from the unhappiness of anger.

One of the most-quoted verses in the Bible is Ephesians 4:26 (NKJV): " 'Be angry, and do not sin' do not let the sun go down on your wrath." My clients uniformly declare that this verse means that their kind of anger is not sin. That may be true. I don't think so. There is a part of that verse that is not debatable. Call your anger righteous if you will; this verse says to get rid of it by sundown.

Just five verses later the apostle Paul clearly states that we can let anger be put away from us (Ephesians 4:31). A few chapters back (Galatians 5:16) we read that people who walk in the Spirit need not struggle with anger, which is a work of the flesh. There is no human remedy. Only God can cleanse your heart.

Remember the quiet man who wanted to atone for his fits of anger by getting up at 5:30 A.M. to read his Bible? Jesus already died to atone for his sins. The man just needed to repent of his bitter, hostile spirit and ask the Lord to forgive and cleanse him and empower him to love his family.

That was a hard pill for him to swallow. It took him a while to give up his favorite reason for his temper. He liked the idea that "he was born that way" so he didn't have to claim responsibility for his temper. He decided to see what would happen if, by faith, he acknowledged his temper to be his responsibility. He asked the Lord for forgiveness and cleansing and strength. Now, he rejoices in his new relationship with the Lord. He is clean, washed, and has a new source of peace and love.

Today, he can lovingly reach for his daughter's hand and patiently remind her to ask someone to pass the bread. Today, he can firmly, but gently, march his son out of the garage, or get the child's attention with a kindly hand to the child's bottom.

I noted a report in our local paper concerning two research projects investigating the effects of hostility:

> "Our studies indicate that hostile, suspicious anger is right up there with any other health hazard we know about, such as cigarette smoking, obesity, and high fat diets," said Dr. Redford Williams of Duke University.[4]

Similar conclusions resulted from two studies begun in the sixties on medical students and law students who were given personality tests in which their hostility was gauged by their reactions to 50 situations.

Researchers found 25 years later that only 4 percent of the lawyers rated basically "easygoing" had died by age 50. But among those ranking in the top quarter of a hostility chart, 20 percent had died.

Among doctors, only 2 percent of the low-hostility types were dead at age 50, compared with 14 percent of their volatile counterparts.

Dr. Mara Williams of the University of Michigan found that women who answered test questions with obvious signs of long-term suppressed anger were three times more likely to have died during her study than those who did not harbor hostile feelings.[5]

These research projects only confirm what the Bible declares: Anger will destroy us. And you can exchange it for love!

9

Is There a Right Kind of Anger?

◆

Almost always when I finish a lecture on anger there is someone in the audience who expresses concern about my "one-sided position" that anger is sin. I also receive lengthy letters sharing that same concern. Their reasoning follows a pattern: Usually the questioner or the letter writer is angry about something and is defending the reasonableness of that anger. They quote the same Bible verses again and again. Here are the verses they quote:

> God gets angry: *"God is a just judge, and God is angry with the wicked every day"* (Psalm 7:11 NKJV).

> Jesus was angry: *"In the temple courts he [Jesus] found men selling cattle, sheep and doves, and others sitting at tables exchanging money. So he*

> *made a whip out of cords, and drove all from the temple area" (John 2:14,15).*

Notice that Jesus had time to make a whip out of cords. That means what He did was not a spontaneous reaction but a planned act. In a recent conference I attended, a man said that God's anger is never occasional, it is eternal. It is resident, not incidental. Likewise, Jesus' anger is never a condition of spontaneous rage. He never became mad as we do. Jesus is eternally angry with sin and eternally forgiving toward sinners.

In Defense of Anger

A flagship verse on anger is Mark 3:1-5. Jesus was in a synagogue and a man with a shriveled hand was there. There were also people who were looking for a reason to accuse Jesus of wrongdoing. They watched closely to see if Jesus would heal on the Sabbath:

> *He looked around at them in anger and, deeply distressed at their stubborn hearts, said to the man, "Stretch out your hand." ... his hand was completely restored (Mark 3:5).*

Those people who justify anger inevitably point to another flagship verse: "'In your anger do not sin': Do not let the sun go down while you are still angry" (Ephesians 4:26).

Using this verse, one letter writer said to me in all-capital letters: BE ANGRY IS A COMMAND.

Another writer, quoting some prestigious authors, made a summary statement of their views:

> Perhaps anger is a God-given emotion that in itself is neither good nor bad. The problem is not the

feeling of anger; the problem with anger is what you do with it. Selfless, disciplined anger in the service of Christ is one of the great dynamic forces of the world. We should be indignant and angry toward the evil in the world.

Was Jesus Really Angry?

I was at a conference center recently. There were three of us sitting around a table—a theologian, a clinical psychologist, and myself. We all agreed that Mark 3:5 states that Jesus was angry.

What, then, we asked ourselves, is godly, Spirit-filled anger like?

We agreed that such anger would take a firm stand against alcoholism, abortion, child abuse, drugs, crime, violence, adultery, fornication, and the breakdown of the family.

Yet a seething, hostile person, fists clenched, the body filled with adrenaline ready to do battle, breathing threats, and thinking destruction is hardly a picture of godly anger. We put those people in hospitals or behind bars. We see to it that they receive tranquilizing medicine.

What can we learn from Mark 3:5, John 2:14,15, and Ephesians 4:26?

First, let's look at the incident involving the cleansing of the temple. The theologian recalled a verse: "Zeal for your house consumes me, and the insults of those who insult you fall on me" (Psalm 69:9).

It is reasonable to conclude that when Jesus used a whip in the temple, He was acting out of zeal for the purity of the church. There is no hint of anger there.

Next we looked at the incident involving the healing of a shriveled hand. Jesus was angry at the people who sought to use a good deed to accuse Him of wrong-doing. Now if all anger is categorically sin, then Jesus sinned. But we know that this is impossible with Jesus. How, then, was Jesus angry without sinning?

Mark 3:5 is the only passage in the New Testament that uses the word "anger" with the person of Christ. However, the word "grief" is also in that same verse. Jesus was angry at their sin *and* grieved at the condition of their hearts. Seldom does someone get angry at people and become grieved over their condition at the same time. Jesus had that ability.

Can We Express Anger?

Our conference discussion began dealing with practical applications, and we took another look at Ephesians 4:26: "'In your anger do not sin': Do not let the sun go down while you are still angry."

Note that we are not commanded to call up anger, but rather, to recognize the sensation of anger whenever it is present within us (the original Greek verb is a present-passive imperative).

We are not to deny the anger; we are not to derive satisfaction from the anger; we are to recognize that it is present and "do not sin."

How do we experience anger and not sin? The same way Jesus experienced anger—if we are walking in union with Him and in the Holy Spirit—by not allowing the sun to go down on the anger nor allowing the devil a foothold. Once we allow anger to become a motivating factor in our lives, the warning in James 1:20 applies: "Man's anger does not bring about the righteous life that God desires."

"Man's anger" in James 1:20 becomes the "fits of

rage" found in Galatians 5:19,20, which lists the deeds of the sinful nature (flesh). Ephesians 4:31 sheds even more light on the issue: "Get rid of all bitterness, rage and anger, brawling and slander, along with every form of malice."

We agreed on the clinical psychologist's observations on these verses. He said that for anger to be "Christ-like," it must fit within the following guidelines.

1. It does not contain an intent to wish harm or bring harm upon the person associated with our anger.

2. It is related to a violation or corruption of God's moral will rather than some "self-determined right."

3. It is briefly experienced but sufficient to motivate toward behavior on our part that is consistent with God's moral will (e.g., acknowledging the anger: "I am feeling angry about the lie you told me. I care about you and our relationship. Will you please tell me the truth from now on?").

4. It is not carried over to the next day and held as a grudge against the person associated with our anger; i.e., we are willing to forgive (live with the consequences of the other person's actions).

A Personal Encounter with Anger

Perhaps you wonder what my response is to these views. I will answer by illustration:

Recently my wife and I were on our way to lecture about this very subject. We went out to rent a car for the trip. I was seated beside the desk of the agent who had to fill out the rental-car form.

Just as we began filling out the form, his phone rang and he talked with a customer about car-rental information. Several more times as we filled out the form the phone rang. I became nervous and looked at my watch. Twenty-five minutes had passed.

Finally I said, "Will you let someone else answer the phone or get someone else to fill out this form!"

Just then my wife walked into the office and overheard my statement. She asked, "What are you upset about?"

"I'm not upset," I shot back. "I'm just trying to get this form filled out."

"You are not being very nice to that poor fellow. Can't you see how busy he is?" she scolded.

"I've been sitting here twenty-five minutes," I tried to explain.

Finally we were on our way. There was a brittle silence between us. I was feeling quite righteous about being ignored by that agent and being misunderstood by my wife.

About half an hour later my cold shoulder toward my wife began to thaw. At last, I could admit that I was angry at that agent and my wife. Neither one of them caused it; their behavior revealed my anger.

When I became aware of my wrongdoing, I realized that if I did not repent on the spot and continued on in that anger it would clearly be sinful. I did repent, and fellowship with my wife was restored and my response to the rental agent was forgiven.

I believe that Ephesians 4:26 is saying that when you are aware of an unloving response to anyone, you should repent on the spot. If there is no repentance, it could lead to other acts of the sinful nature.

A Word of Caution

Psychology books classify both anger and joy as emotions.

Yet in the Bible, anger (literally, "fits of rage," which, by the way, is not the Greek word translated "anger" in Mark 3:5) is called a work of the flesh. Joy is called a fruit of the Spirit.

Anger as a work of the flesh is always sin. There is no human remedy. Only when you live by the Spirit will you not gratify the desire of the sinful nature (Galatians 5:16).

You cannot merely decide to become angry. Sooner or later, your anger is triggered. When you are aware of anger in your body, you will be forced to do something to manage that anger.

The Christian has two options. You can repent (recognizing that anger is sin) and yield yourself to the cleansing and empowering ministry of the Holy Spirit. Or, you can attempt to manage the anger in your sinful heart yourself. You can learn to manage your anger without giving God a thought. There are skilled therapists who can help you. It's self-control versus a lifetime dependence on Spirit control. These are opposites.

Remember Mr. Hartley? A cursing employee triggered his anger (sin). A therapist could help Hartley learn how to change from expressing his anger in destructive ways and develop new behavior patterns that will enable him to express his anger in constructive, satisfying ways.

Tragically, many Christians turn to therapy (humanism) for relief from a sinful heart instead of turning to God for a cure.

To repeat, God commands us to walk in His Spirit. We are ordered to love evil people. If I were supposed to be angry at all the evil I encounter, I would be angry most of the time.

Replacing Anger with Love

A certain couple came to visit me. The lady sat there seething with animosity toward her husband. She had just learned that he had been unfaithful to her throughout their 30-year marriage. There were dozens of other women involved. Her husband sat there looking very contrite. He had a long history of deception, hypocrisy, and satisfying his lusts.

He claimed to be genuinely repentant. No one would believe him. They said he was only sorry he got caught. He said his wife, who was normally a pleasant person, had become an angry, hateful, unresponsive person. She said it was his fault. He didn't know what more he could do. He wanted to know if I believed him.

My answer? "God loves both of you enough to have sacrificed His Son for your sins and to give you access to the fruit of the Spirit. I love both of you, too, but I have no way of knowing the condition of your hearts."

The good news is that her husband's behavior could not come between her and God. She could call on God at any time and exchange her animosity for love, joy, peace, and kindness. All were available for the asking. Of course, she would still need to deal with her marital problem—even after a change of heart.

Her husband had the same access to God. He could exchange his sins for the fruit of the Spirit.

I have seen others sitting in the same chairs:

- A woman unfaithful to her husband
- A man who beat his wife's face into a swollen black-and-blue mess

- A couple who swindled some widows of tens of thousands of dollars
- A teenage thief who is on drugs or alcohol
- A man tormented by the memory of raping and killing a woman
- A woman who walked away from her husband and children
- A teacher who sexually abused some students
- A couple who disagreed over money, social life, or how to manage children.

I can go on and on. The range of human behavior because of sinful hearts seems endless. I suppose the most serious are couples and parents who neglect each other and their children.

God loves them all; none of these people deserve it. They are all sinners—just a prayer away from a new start.

If there is any basis for anger here, it would be toward those people who decide to turn their backs on accepting God's solution and a lifetime of dependence on the Holy Spirit.

A Plan for Repentance

Jesus died for the president of the United States, the members of Congress, governors, mayors, judges, lawyers, stockbrokers, CEOs, drug dealers, alcohol and tobacco manufacturers, prostitutes, pornography dealers, men, women, and children.

Why? Because He loved them!

Repentance for anger as sin is rare. Jesus explained why:

This is the verdict: Light has come into the world, but men loved darkness instead of light because their deeds were evil. Everyone who does evil hates the light, and will not come into the light for fear that his deeds will be exposed (John 3:19,20).

Unrepentant, intelligent people believe that they can justify their anger because God gets angry. This is why they comb the Gospels for any shred of evidence that Jesus got angry. The term "righteous indignation" just blurs the issue.

Perhaps 95 percent of anyone's anger is plain, old-fashioned sin and we all know it. Anger plagues everyone. We should simply face it and take Jesus up on His offer: "Come to me all you who are weary and burdened, and I will give you rest" (Matthew 11:28).

As I wrote this book, my good friend Homer Dowdy read this chapter. I pass on his comments about God's anger:

God's perfect holiness, His utter righteousness, are so far removed from us in our sinful condition that when we speak of God's anger and our anger, even our "righteous indignation," we cannot use the same language for both. Even though the word "anger" may be the same in both texts, the meaning of each is as different as light is from darkness, good is from evil, the Creator is from His creation. ("My thoughts are not your thoughts, neither are your ways my ways, saith the LORD" [Isaiah 55:8 KJV].) Until we are in God's presence, we cannot fully understand His ways, His expressions. Extend God's anger to the ultimate and you get what Jonathan

Edwards called zeal. Extend any anger employed by fallible man and you get something tainted, which is what you could expect from one who in this life can see only through a glass, darkly.

10

Dealing with a Child's Anger

◆

The Bible gives parents a very sobering assignment:

> *Fathers, do not provoke your children to wrath, but bring them up in the training and admonition of the Lord (Ephesians 6:4 NKJV).*

The J.B. Phillips translation of the New Testament puts another emphasis to the task:

> *Fathers, don't overcorrect your children or make it difficult for them to obey the commandment. Bring them up with Christian teaching in Christian discipline (Ephesians 6:4 PHILLIPS).*

In the same passage is some advice for children as well:

> *Obey your parents in the Lord, for this is right.*
> *"Honor your father and mother"—which is the first*
> *commandment with a promise—"that it may go well*
> *with you and that you may enjoy long life on the earth"*
> *(Ephesians 6:1-3).*

Children in Rebellion

One summer I worked with a mission organization that placed a team of college students in Indian villages located on some of the islands along the coastline of British Columbia. We spent a month in the village, offering a recreation program for the children during the day and Bible studies for the adults in the evenings. My responsibility was to move from island to island to supervise these students.

Mike

One of the students (whom I'll call Mike) and I were sitting on a log one evening watching a spectacular sunset. I was glorying in the magnificent scene when Mike broke the silence with a pathetic story about his alcoholic father. (Alcoholism was a serious problem with the Indians.)

His dad would come home drunk almost weekly and break furniture and dishes and beat up his wife. The children would scatter to stay out of the way. His dad died several years ago, which should have removed him from the scene. Yet when Mike slows down enough to be quiet, he recalls his father and is consumed by bitterness, hatred, and anger. This was his response to a magnificent sunset.

I read to Mike the verses in Ephesians 6:1-4. He responded to the words, "Fathers, do not provoke your children to wrath." The reason he gave for his hostile spirit was the treatment he received from his father. I told him that such an attitude would be true of a humanist, but the Christian has a resource that transforms an angry heart into a loving heart: "The love of God has been poured out in our hearts by the Holy Spirit who was given to us" (Romans 5:5 NKJV).

Mike didn't want to change his heart even if he had God's love available. He preferred to stew over his memories and was convinced that his father caused the bitter hatred in his heart. He had never had anyone question his response, and his Christian friends sympathized with and supported him.

I asked Mike if he accepted the thought that God loves him. He readily embraced that, and added, "Warts and all my faults included."

I wondered if Mike agreed that God loves these alcoholic, mean, and violent Indians? He agreed. Would Mike advise the children in this village to love their violent, alcoholic fathers? The obvious answer is yes; the Bible says, "Honor your father and mother . . . that it may go well with you and that you may enjoy long life on the earth" (Ephesians 6:2,3).

"Mike," I said, "do you realize that you can't even enjoy this sunset because you refuse to allow the Holy Spirit in you to do His work?"

Silence enveloped us. It seemed to last forever. I thought I heard Mike sobbing. He came to this island to tell these people that God loved them. He loved them too, but he hated his father. He told himself it was his father's fault, but now began to realize the hate came from his own sinful heart.

"I did it. I did it. Now I love my dad," Mike shouted.

We hugged each other and celebrated together. He fought a battle with the law of sin and wound up with love in his heart.

Poor Mike had carried an unnecessary burden for several years because the Christian teaching he received was tainted with a dash of humanism (the law of sin). He was taught that he was a victim of his dad's alcoholism, which accounted for the hatred and anger in his heart. He thought he was mistreated, not sinful.

Pete

The next day another teammate (I'll call him Pete) approached me following a conversation with Mike. He asked about Ephesians 6:1, which says, "Obey your parents in the Lord, for this is right."

Pete's parents divorced. His father remarried, so now he had a stepmother. His mother remarried, so now he had a stepfather. His father divorced again and now has a live-in partner. They omitted the marriage ceremony altogether.

With a belligerent spirit, Pete wanted to know which of these people he should obey. He was not alone in this dilemma; there are millions of children caught in the swirling, ungodly behavior of their parents. These children can justify any kind of behavior if they choose to consider themselves victims of an impossible environment.

"How can I honor these people?" grumbled Pete.

How do you answer an impossible question like that? A verse in the book of Romans came to mind: "But God demonstrates his own love for us in this: While we were still sinners, Christ died for us" (Romans 5:8).

Jesus loved those people who dumped Pete into a

hopelessly confusing mess, but Pete found it hard to love them. Yet, here he was, a Christian, witnessing of his faith in an Indian village, discussing this problem with me. It was necessary for Pete to sort out the law of sin in his thinking. The humanists would say that Pete has a cesspool of hidden feelings deep in his heart, and it will take a long period of skillful probing to root them out. This process does not involve God.

Not so. Jesus will cleanse his heart of all unrighteousness. Even though Pete's parents were sinful, he needed to love them and honor them. Obviously, he must look elsewhere for guidance. He must look to the law of the spirit of life in Christ. As a child of God, he can do as the apostle Paul did:

> *And be found in him, not having a righteousness of my own that comes from the law, but that which is through faith in Christ—the righteousness that comes from God and is by faith (Philippians 3:9).*

That truth helped Pete realize in a flash that God was looking after him.

Marvin

Marvin was another mission-student teammate. He came from a stable, predictable Christian home. He grew up in the church. He was spared all the turmoil that Mike and Pete had to endure. But Marvin created his own problems. In his teens he longed to abandon the church and run with some friends at school who came from backgrounds similar to Mike and Pete's. That side of the tracks seemed so much more exciting than the stable home and lifestyle he was saddled with. It does not follow that a good home guarantees a contented, cooperative child.

Marvin's parents were united in their insistence that he stay with the church, choose wholesome activities, choose decent friends, keep reasonable hours, and keep up with his schoolwork. Fortunately, his resistance did not upset them. His threats of abandoning their way of life did not move them. When he finally came to his senses, they rejoiced with him.

Mike and Pete were struggling with a hostile spirit toward problem parents. Marvin had struggles with a rebellious spirit toward stable, spiritual parents.

All three students were struggling with the works of the flesh—their sinful nature. Their interaction with their families revealed the condition of their hearts. So each one had two problems: 1) what to do about the condition underneath his own skin; 2) how to respond to his parents.

Dealing with a sinful nature requires young people to deal directly with God. He will cleanse them from their sins and empower them to walk in the Spirit.

Responding to problem parents requires children to interact with the parents to negotiate a livable plan.

Mike, Pete, and Marvin all had a month to practice what they learned with other friends who were learning to walk in the Spirit—all in an environment pervaded by alcoholism and violence.

Parental Responsibility

So far we have been looking at a child's response to problem parents. What about the parents' responsibility to the child? The Bible says, "Fathers, do not provoke your children to wrath, but bring them up in the training and admonition of the Lord" (Ephesians 6:4 NKJV).

The Bible declares that hate, anger, and resentment are the results of the sinful nature. If so, then parents are part of the problem or the solution in family strife. They are responsible to provide an environment where 1) their children are taught how to be cleansed from sin and walk in the Spirit, and 2) their lives put into practice what they teach.

A fundamental truth is that strife between members of a family is not *produced* by circumstances, it is *revealed* by them. Parents must seek to provide an environment that allows God to work in the lives of their children. Three key steps are involved:

Personal Preparation

Proverbs 4:23 encourages us with these words: "Above all else, guard your heart, for it is the wellspring of life."

You must see to it that you eat properly, exercise, and get enough sleep. No one else can do these for you. Likewise, you must look after your own heart.

Acts of the Sinful Nature

Ephesians 5:18 says, "Do not get drunk on wine. . . . Instead, be filled with the Spirit." A person who gets drunk is declared to be under the influence of alcohol. Likewise, a person who commits acts of the sinful nature can be declared to be "under the influence of the law of sin." The acts of the sinful nature are obvious:

> *Sexual immorality, impurity and debauchery;*
> *idolatry and witchcraft; hatred, discord, jealousy,*
> *fits of rage, selfish ambition, dissensions, factions*

and envy; drunkenness, orgies, and the like (Galatians 5:19-21).

Without a doubt, some of these acts of the sinful nature have become manifest in your behavior at one time or another. You have two options for dealing with them:

1. *You can learn to live with your sinful nature.* If necessary, you can seek help from skilled therapists who have made a study of how to manage "human behavior" (acts of the sinful nature).

2. *You can turn Godward.* Jesus died and rose again so that He could cleanse your sin. There is no human remedy for sin. You must come to Jesus alone. No one can force you or hinder you. The Bible points the way:

Who will rescue me from this body of death? Thanks be to God—through Jesus Christ our Lord! (Romans 7:24,25).

God made him who had no sin to be sin for us, so that in him we might become the righteousness of God (2 Corinthians 5:21).

Live by the Spirit, and you will not gratify the desires of the sinful nature (Galatians 5:16).

The Fruit of the Spirit

A person "filled with the Spirit" possesses love, joy, peace, patience, kindness, goodness, faithfulness, gentleness and self-control (Galatians 5:22,23).

A person who responds to the events of each day "filled with the Spirit" can be claimed to be "under the influence of the Holy Spirit." Of course, we know that to respond "in the Spirit" is an impossibility, humanly speaking. But with God, help is only a prayer away. The source is the Holy Spirit.

To respond to the demands of each day "in the Spirit" simply requires that you depend on God for the rest of your life.

Mothers and fathers who seek to walk in the Spirit are contributing to an environment that will allow God to work in the lives of their children. This is the most valuable influence parents could possibly have.

The second step in allowing God to work in the lives of your children is . . .

Teamwork

Guiding children requires teamwork. The Bible says:

Submit to one another out of reverence for Christ (Ephesians 5:21).

Wives, submit to your husbands as to the Lord (Ephesians 5:22).

Husbands, love your wives, just as Christ loved the church (Ephesians 5:25).

Occasionally I hear parents say they must put up a united front. *These verses require united hearts.* To meet this requirement calls for transformation, not conformity. Spouses who wish to submit to one another can follow this model: "[Be] like-minded, having the same love, being one in spirit and purpose" (Philippians 2:2).

If your minds are not together, then you are not together. To function in a truly united way will require guidelines for all areas of your lives, including the use of money, eating, housekeeping, hygiene, clothing, social life, church life, and relating to each other's families. As long as you keep up this process, you will contribute to creating an environment where God can work through your family.

The third essential parents need to provide for children is . . .

Guidance

Raising children is a 20-year process and requires the utmost cooperation between parents. The objective is found in an often-quoted and much-discussed Bible verse: "Train a child in the way he should go, and when he is old he will not turn from it" (Proverbs 22:6).

To carry out this 20-year minimum responsibility implies a Spirit-filled woman and man who join their lives together in marriage. They are voluntarily committed to maintaining a meeting of their minds during a lifetime of constant change—all because of their reverence for Christ. Together they will study their children and spend enough time together with them so they are aware of each child's talents, abilities, interests, and physical development. They will establish reasonable guidelines that, according to their judgment, fit the children and change as the family grows and circumstances dictate. By faith they assume that the wisdom and judgment they need will come out of their mutual reverence for Christ. In doing all this, they are creating an environment where God can work in their children.

There are two statements that I like (and unfortunately, I do not know the sources):

- The best way to teach character is to have it around the house.

- Much of what you give your children is caught, not taught.

Family life consists mostly of performing the usual routines day in and day out. In the process, parents naturally interact with their children. The Bible provides some insights on interaction:

> *The Lord's servant must not quarrel; instead, he must be kind to everyone, able to teach, not resentful. Those who oppose him he must gently instruct, in the hope that God will grant them repentance leading them to a knowledge of the truth, and that they will come to their senses and escape from the trap of the devil, who has taken them captive to do his will (2 Timothy 2:24-26).*

I would like to add two nonverbal convictions as well: "Follow my example, as I follow the example of Christ" (1 Corinthians 11:1), and, "Whatever you have learned or received or heard from me, or seen in me— put it into practice. And the God of peace will be with you" (Philippians 4:9).

You cannot force your children to follow your example, but you can, by your example, show how becoming Christlike is possible and beneficial.

In Review...

1. Children ought to have parents who model the Christian life for them. They should have the benefit of biblically oriented training and instruction.

2. Children should obey such training.

3. Children are on the road to enjoying long life on earth if they honor their parents.

---

4. Good role modeling and proper training from parents is no substitute for needing a Savior and Lord. All have sinned, including children.

5. We all ended up at the same starting line, even though we arrive from different directions (remember Mike, Pete, and Marvin?).

6. All the resources of God are available to every one of us.

11

Perfect Love Eliminates Fear

◆

Occasionally I've been asked to help someone who is struggling with strange, mysterious fears. A highly skilled craftsman is suddenly overcome with the fear that he has lost his ability and would surely fail if he tried to return to work. A very gracious hostess suddenly can't face people for fear of offending them. A man who drives 60,000 miles a year is terrified at the thought of flying in an airplane. None of these people have a scrap of evidence to explain their fears.

The Bible verse that speaks most specifically about fear seems to say that fearfulness is the product of faulty love toward someone: "There is no fear in love. But perfect love drives out fear, because fear has to do with punishment. The man who fears is not made perfect in love" (1 John 4:18).

That is strong language. It implies that love and

hate do not exist in the heart at the same time. That makes sense. According to the Bible (Galatians 5:19-23), love is a fruit of the Spirit and hate is a work of the flesh. Then it follows that love does not coexist with anger, resentment, bitterness, rebellion, and other such emotions. If that's true, the biblical principle makes sense when it says, *"Perfect love drives out fear."* In other words, the awareness of fear can be a signal to you to deal with some hatred or anger that blocks the love of God from flooding your heart.

A Mysterious Battle with Fear

A lady approached me after a meeting. She wondered what she could do about a growing feeling of inadequacy and a crippling fear of failure. She related to me that she was a singer. But lately, whenever she sang, her body stiffened up, her vocal cords felt strained, and the fear of missing a note gripped her.

I needed more information. Did she have a history of making mistakes while singing? No, she never made mistakes. My oh my, she would die if she made a mistake. How good was she? Her singing was mostly for Sunday morning church services. She was considered the best singer available in the church (her husband was the minister). Did she really never make a mistake? Never. There was just the fear of making a mistake.

That didn't make sense to me. Here was a person who was afraid of failing at something she had never failed. She had been singing for years and loving it. The delight of her life was to sing. But now she dreaded the thought of singing, and at a time in her life when she had been performing at her very best.

There was no doubt that she had these anxiety attacks, but it didn't seem to me that the cause could be a sense of inferiority. She firmly rejected the *fact* of inferiority; she only *felt* inferior.

My reflection on the subject of love came to my mind. Could it be that she was mad at someone? The Bible says that perfect love eliminates fear. Perhaps her problem was unrelated to singing. But, said the woman, the only time she felt this way was when she sang. That was enough of a problem without my adding to it.

As I pressed her to at least consider the principle of perfect love casting out fear, she turned on her heel and left. It seemed like I had really blown that one; she was more disturbed when she left than when she had come.

Recovery from Fear

About a year later, a lady approached me and asked, "Do you remember me?" She appeared to be relaxed and cheerful. It was the same lady who had the singing problem. She was eager to bring me up-to-date.

When she had left after our talk a year ago, she was upset. As she drove home, it became clear to her that she was very angry at me. She couldn't deny that. It became equally clear to her that she was mad at her husband. That opened a floodgate.

The story is that her husband had accepted this pastorate about two years ago. In the previous church, whenever the choir needed a female soloist, she was always the one selected. The church family loved to hear her sing. But at this new church, the music director chose a variety of soloists, all of them with lesser ability than she had. She called this to her husband's attention but he refused to interfere. So she was nursing an angry spirit toward both her husband and the music director.

The Sunday-school class that she wanted to join

had an entrance requirement. The combined age of a couple could not exceed 80 years. She didn't qualify. So now she was mad at about 40 people in the class, plus her husband, plus the music director.

Later, the church had an annual family banquet. She was asked to be in charge. She chose a fine hotel for the banquet, but that night the banquet room was too hot, the meal was mediocre, and the sound system didn't work. Many people were unhappy with the banquet.

"Who put this one together?" they asked.

"The pastor's wife," came the response.

She resented the criticism aimed at her, and as a result, she became hostile toward all 800 members of the church, plus her husband, and the music director. That's 802 people! And this was the audience to whom she would sing. Is it any wonder that she would stiffen up and her vocal cords would become strained?

All alone in her car on the way home, she began to realize the problem that was inside of her. She repented of her ugly spirit and asked the Lord to forgive her and clean up her heart and fill it with His love. She was happy to report that her fear was now gone. Her problem? Imperfect love. Only God could help her, help which she gladly received when she saw her need.

What is imperfect love? It is a hatred toward someone. This imperfect love, or hatred, brings fear. Perfect love, or God, casts out fear!

One day a lady told me that an audiotape message about the singer's experience helped her to solve a problem. Her husband was a leader in a Christian organization. His work involved considerable travel. She often traveled with him and gave lectures to women on how to live the Spirit-filled life. She eventually noticed that she was becoming fearful of taking off and landing in an airplane. She noticed the same dread when riding in elevators.

Dreading an upcoming trip, she listened to the tape, thinking that she could get some help for herself. She reported that as she listened a second time, there were two relationships in which she was involved that came into her mind. There was no doubt that her response to both people was anger. She had been ignoring or justifying her response. Now she saw it as sin that blocked the love of God from her heart. She repented on the spot. There was no noticeable change of which she was aware. She was busy and had other things on her mind, so her concern about her fears took a backseat.

Later, as she and her husband took off in an airplane, it dawned on her that she was not afraid. She was very alert during the landing and was astounded that her enjoyment of flying was back. Afterward, while she was in an elevator, she noted that her fear was gone. And now, she wanted me to know that she had found relief from her struggles with fear by means of a cassette tape delivered to her by a concerned friend.

Are All Fears the Result of Sin?

The obvious question that surrounds these strange fears is this: Is *all* fear because of hidden sin?

An editor who read this chapter noted that, after all, there are fears that help us act cautiously when driving on icy roads, hiking up a steep mountain trail, or walking on a wet sidewalk. Very true. In fact, if a person was not cautious when driving on an icy road or walking on a wet sidewalk, that would be cause for concern.

I recall sitting in an airplane for two hours until someone could de-ice the wings of the plane. We would have had good reason for concern if the pilot had insisted on taking off without de-icing the plane. But it would not make sense to worry about all future flights for fear of ice forming on the wings.

One morning my wife and I were walking along in an airport and the next thing I knew, she was sprawled flat on her back on the floor. At that point she hardly looked like her carefully groomed self. She had slipped on a wet floor that had just been mopped.

Thus it makes sense for Jo to be careful when walking on airport floors. But if she refused to leave the house again for fear that she would slip and fall, that wouldn't make sense.

One year in our county, 13 children drowned in private swimming pools during the month of July. It makes good sense for parents to be concerned about proper supervision of small children around private pools.

However, the singer who was fearful of making a mistake had no logical reason for her fear. The lady who was afraid of airplanes and elevators could not logically explain her fear. Both had panic attacks to be sure, but they had no reason to be afraid.

Therapists call these panic attacks "phobias." A phobia is an obsessing (repeated), morbid fear or dread from which a person cannot escape.

No facts, no information, no clarification, no reassurance will change the person's response. Why? Because that's the wrong way to deal with the problem. The Bible says, "The man who fears is not made perfect in love" (1 John 4:18).

The first question to ask when an unrealistic fear persists is, Who am I mad at? The people I cited earlier were denying their anger, but it came out in the form of panic attacks in odd places and at odd times. In the case of the singer, her anger toward the whole church flared when she stood before them to sing. Her deceitful heart, however, convinced her that feelings of inferiority caused her to fear singing. What a lie!

The lady who was afraid of flying was quietly fuming over the behavior of two other people. Yet her deceitful heart convinced her that she was tense and anxious because she was afraid of airplanes.

It seems that in their search for peace from anxiety, people will do anything but try to understand what sin is.

I told the stories about the two fearful ladies at a conference. Afterward, a lady asked to talk with me. She was one the sponsors of the conference and was the type of person who would stand out in any group—well-groomed, beautiful, well-dressed, and charming. After a few minutes of conversation with her I could tell that she was a well-educated person. Indeed, she was a leader in the community, conducting seminars on marriage and the family. She and her husband were considered to be exemplary as a couple and a family. Her husband was owner of a thriving business.

My lecture disturbed her because she abhorred flying. She understood me to be saying that her fear meant that she could be angry at someone.

I told her, yes, that is what I said. I added that there are some legitimate reasons for fear, and asked her if she had some negative experiences associated with flying. Since there were none, I suggested that her fear of flying had no basis.

"Perhaps you're feeling hostile toward someone," I told her. "Why not think about it and meet me later?"

We set up an appointment.

A serious-looking lady showed up. In retrospection she "discovered" a problem that had been going on for years. It involved her and her husband. She had resented some of his ways since the beginning of their marriage. For example, he was color-blind and frequently didn't match colors in his attire. She also didn't like the way he talked about women. And his treatment of her and the children really got to her. But she was a strong advocate of a wife being in subjection to her husband, so she learned to live with his ways. He didn't even know how she felt.

I replied that she was not submitting to her husband; she was only appearing to be submissive. I asked, "What are you doing when you pretend to accept his ways?"

She thought about that for a while, and then sheepishly called her behavior deceptive and hypocritical. She needed to give her tension a reason, and one day she chose airplanes.

Her behavior is described in the Bible:

> *The heart is deceitful above all things and beyond cure. Who can understand it? "I the LORD search the heart and examine the mind, to reward a man according to his conduct, according to what his deeds deserve" (Jeremiah 17:9,10).*

This woman had denied this truth all these years. She now received this new insight into her heart; it was up to her to continue as she was or to repent.

She left. Later I received a letter from her. It said that our talk lanced a pocket of sin filled with unresolved bitterness. She was so ashamed that she almost left the conference. She confessed the bitterness as sin on her way to the chapel on the conference grounds. She then experienced a renewed love for her husband, which has continued since.

In her letter she wrote:

> Now the good news. We just returned from a trip. I enjoyed it. In fact, the Lord placed a lady beside me who was petrified. I shared the *Four Spiritual Laws* with her. Her response was, "Can you think of anything more wonderful?" She prayed to ask the Lord to save her. She said, "I was waiting for the stewardess to come along so I could buy three or four martinis to get me to my destination, but now I have no fear."
>
> There is more. On the way home, I fell asleep, and sitting in a window seat at that. Needless to say, this is a miracle of God.

Since receiving that letter, I have listened to many weary people who were struggling with unrealistic fears. They were obsessed. By definition, an obsession is a persistent feeling or idea which a person cannot escape.

A Proper Response to Fear

Below is a list of some of the fears that people have expressed to me but could not back up with a reasonable explanation:

driving	offending others
crowds	children's safety
elevators	germs
airplanes	making decisions
heights	authority
failure or inadequacy	drowning in a shower stall

All of these people had the same experience. When they saw that there was no reasonable explanation for their fear, but rather that their problem was an obsession, they were ready to consider this biblical principle: *Perfect love eliminates fear.*

Then they could look in their hearts and find hate, anger, resentment, or rebellion that was being denied and follow the biblical course: *confession of sin, repentance, and God's empowerment.*

Every Christian needs to be familiar with this process.

The University of Florida established a "Fear and Anxiety" clinic in 1981. In 1993, after 12 years of research, Bruce Cuthbert explained that they might have had better therapies if they had understood the disorders better. Some scientists believe that fears of snakes, spiders, and heights might be survival instincts that go back in time. They reason that snakes were deadly to ancestors living in the wild, and monkeys are also afraid of snakes. They guess that the fear of heights originated when Og the Caveman tumbled from a cliff. (It takes a lot of faith to follow that logic.)

Experts are puzzled, he says, by the current rash of panic attacks and the growing number of agoraphobics (people who posses a morbid fear toward being in an open place). In 1950 there were no agoraphobics. Then there were a few reported in England, and now they are all over.[1]

I call on Christians to pray for these sincere researchers who believe that our anxieties might be survival instincts that date from caveman days. Be careful to test their conclusions against God's Word.

12

Enjoying the Spirit of Life in Christ

Romans 8:2 states an incredible truth about the freedom we as believers can enjoy in Christ: "Through Christ Jesus the law of the Spirit of life set me free from the law of sin and death" (Romans 8:2).

The law of sin pulls us downward. It causes us to miss the mark that we set for ourselves. The law of the Spirit of life in Christ Jesus, however, pulls us upward.

As we discovered earlier, the Bible describes the fruit of the Spirit as "love, joy, peace, patience, kindness, goodness, faithfulness, gentleness and self-control. Against such things there is no law" (Galatians 5:22,23).

You cannot pass a law that forces me to love you or to have a heart filled with joy. You cannot order me to be a peaceful man. You can force me to *act* like I love you.

You can determine how a joyful person should *look* and require everyone to look that way.

But you cannot pass a law that orders me to cease being angry, hateful, or lustful. You can only pass a law that limits the way I can behave when I am angry, or hateful, or lustful.

John Milton wrote in *Areopagitica* (1644, an argument for freedom of the press) a great description of a person wailing in the flesh:

> Wherefore did He create passions within us, pleasures round about us, but that these rightly tempered are the very ingredients of virtue? They are not skillful considerers of human things, who imagine to remove sin by removing the matter of sin. Thou ye take from covetous man all his treasure, he has yet one jewel left, ye cannot bereave him of his covetousness. Banish all objects of lust, shut up all youth in the severest of discipline that can be exercised in any hermitage, ye cannot make them chaste, that came not thither so. This justifies the high providence of God, who, though He command us temperance, justice, continence, yet pours before us, even to a profuseness, all desirable things, and gives us minds that wander beyond all limit and satiety.[1]

You cannot legislate the condition of anyone's heart. There is a vast difference between a cheerful manner and a cheerfulness that emanates from the Spirit.

There are controlling mechanisms in the body that cannot be resisted. It is possible to control some parts of the body by exercising willpower. Breathing, pulse rate, and bowel functions are examples. But the demands of the body eventually take over.

Likewise, we can control our emotions and behaviors to some extent by willpower. But soon the body takes over. For example:

- I decide to eat no more desserts.

- I decide to quit lying.

- I decide to stop being angry at my parents.

Personal resolve can melt like chocolate bars in the sun when you are standing in front of a well-stocked dessert bar. Selfishness can compel you to lie your way out of going shopping. Parental insistence on cleaning up the bedroom can make you furious. Unconditional love disappears.

Students of human behavior observe that our responses are shaped by social interaction. That is true to some extent.

Biblically oriented observers of human behavior recognize two laws that govern our lives: the law of sin, and the law of the Spirit of life in Christ Jesus.

Overcoming the Law of Sin

We have some choice over which law prevails in life, just as we have some choice over obeying physical laws. For example, as I mentioned in chapter 3, I have a broken tooth that reminds me to respect the law of gravity.

There is another law that overcomes the law of gravity; it's called the law of aerodynamics. I wrote part of this book flying through the air at 33,000 feet. The construction and operation of the contraption in which I sat was very complicated. I knew nothing about it. Yet all I need to do to overcome the law of gravity is to entrust my life to the pilots of the plane. If the plane engines were to stop running, the law of gravity would take over and the plane would crash to the ground.

The law of the Spirit of life in Christ Jesus is like the law of aerodynamics. This law overcomes the law of sin as long as you submit to the law of the Spirit of life in Christ Jesus. Note that the law of sin doesn't go away; rather it is suspended. The Bible says:

> For what the law was powerless to do in that it was weakened by the sinful nature, God did by sending his own Son in the likeness of sinful man to be a sin offering. And so he condemned sin in sinful man, in order that the righteous requirements of the law might be fully met in us, who do not live according to the sinful nature but according to the Spirit (Romans 8:3,4).

To live up to the law of the Spirit requires a supernatural miracle. In order to experience the fruit of the Spirit, you must first understand that these qualities are just that—the result of yielding to the Spirit of God. If it is true that these qualities are the result of yielding to the Spirit of God in you, then you are forced to conclude that they are not affected by your interaction with people. Nor are they affected by your interaction with the circumstances of life. *People and circumstances will reveal your spirit, not cause it.*

In other words, we do not produce a consistent pattern of Spirit-filled behavior by means of training, determination, willpower, good intentions, or self-control. You don't need to take my word for it; simply observe yourself and pay attention to your reactions to other people as well as your circumstances.

Making Choices

My wife and I were driving along Interstate 95 through Florida on a beautiful, sunny afternoon. We were chatting pleasantly. The cruise control was set at 55 miles per hour and we were in the middle lane. A car on the left whizzed past us and suddenly swerved into our lane. I had to stomp quickly on the brakes to prevent a nasty accident. My wife didn't see the incident but she felt the effect of the brakes, which caused her body to lurch forward. I calmly told her what had happened. Together we watched that car weave in and out of different lanes until it was out of sight.

Later that day I recalled the incident. It dawned on me that when that car swerved in front of me, I had to make a split-second decision to either walk in the Spirit or in the flesh. That I responded peacefully with a kind attitude toward that driver was a miracle. I could recall similar instances when, in a split second, I was transformed into an angry man with my heart pounding, my body alert, and a stream of nasty words tumbling out of my mouth.

We make many such split-second decisions every day. Without our noticing, other people make choices that affect us and force us into making a decision. We have no control of the incidents around us, but we do determine whether to yield to the Spirit or to the flesh.

When I note that I yield to the Spirit instead of the flesh, I do so with a sense of grateful relief. How positively wonderful it is to know that I no longer need to manage myself by myself! Now I can let God do it—per His request. Take it to the Lord in prayer; He will never leave you nor forsake you. The Bible says, "It is God who works in you to will and to act according to his good purpose" (Philippians 2:13).

Consistent living, then, is a matter of recognizing your own personal inability to produce the kind of spirit that you want, no matter how intense your desire. It involves receiving and yielding to the Spirit of Christ.

By the strength of your willpower, you can speak and behave properly. It's your spirit that you can't manage. It's not changing standards and rules that transforms a person. A change of heart is needed.

The Bible explains this clearly: The apostle Paul said he wanted to "be found in [Christ], not having a righteousness of my own that comes from the law, but that which is through faith in Christ—the righteousness that comes from God and is by faith" (Philippians 3:9).

Paul was seeking to cultivate a spirit that would enable him to conform to a reasonable law so that what he said or did was a reflection of what was in his heart. In his letter to the Corinthians, he called the Holy Spirit a treasure and described how we could respond to the events of life:

> We have this treasure in jars of clay to show that this all-surpassing power is from God and not from us. We are hard pressed on every side, but not crushed; perplexed, but not in despair; persecuted, but not abandoned; struck down, but not destroyed (2 Corinthians 4:7-9).

From Hostility to Peace

I had a conversation with a man following a speech I gave about these verses. I had said there is a power that will enable a person who is troubled, perplexed, or persecuted to deal with his situation without distress or despair—and without feeling forsaken or cast down.

This man (let's call him Mr. Black) was an engineer. He designed and built some of the equipment that harnessed atomic energy and made possible the bomb that was dropped over Hiroshima. He had a great awe and respect for the tremendous power of the atom. But for years he was a troubled man, in conflict with his boss, who frequently changed Mr. Black's designs apparently without careful study. As a result, sometimes the equipment worked well when it was built, and sometimes it didn't. When it worked well, his boss took the credit. When the equipment failed, Mr. Black got the blame. He said nothing, but became a bitter man. These bottled-up resentments resulted in tormented, sleepless nights during which he endlessly reviewed his grudges toward his boss. He also suffered remorse over his cruel words and deeds that made life miserable for his wife and children.

One day, when his boss insisted on a change with which Mr. Black disagreed, he slammed his fist on the desk and vented his wrath on his boss. He flatly refused to work for him another day. It was an embarrassing temper tantrum, and he was unceremoniously transferred to another department.

As the weeks went by, Mr. Black developed the same trouble in the new department. His new boss pushed him to get the work done faster. Mr. Black felt they were working too rapidly, and again the tension began to build up within him.

"Slowly it began to dawn on me that perhaps I was wrong," he told me. "As I looked back on my past, I had to admit that this bottled-up rebellion had plagued me most of my life. I began to see that I needed to change and I searched the Bible in hope of finding an answer."

He found it:

> *Whatever you do, work at it with all your heart, as working for the Lord, not for men, since you know that you will receive an inheritance from the Lord as a reward. It is the Lord Christ you are serving. Anyone who does wrong will be repaid for his wrong, and there is no favoritism (Colossians 3:23-25).*

"Upon reading this I broke out in a sweat and began to tremble," Mr. Black continued. "I realized that I was acting like a little boy, sulking at my drawing board and venting my wrath on innocent people. It was a relief to see this and admit it. My heart turned to God in repentance with a prayer for the power to act like a man, to do my work heartily, to serve God, and to let other men's decisions rest with God. Ten years later, my boss still pressures me and changes my designs, but work is now pleasant."

Before his discovery, Mr. Black was bitter, rebellious, hostile, and wrathful. Then he turned to God, began depending on God's power, and work became pleasant. Mr. Black was at ease, relaxed.

This man, who had learned how to harness the destructive power of atomic energy, had also learned about the destructive power of bottled-up resentment. He learned that he couldn't bottle up the Spirit of God, but he could walk in Him day by day. As a result, the power of God changed his reactions to life.

People who seek help from counselors are driven to them because they suffer torment that is sometimes beyond what a human can endure. If not given help, many would break down completely. This torment is the result of hate, rebellion, indignation, anger, bitterness, desperation, guilt, resentment, cruelty, or remorse—an "internal" struggle causing tension and often sleeplessness.

Shifting the Blame

Note that these are the reactions of talented, well-educated, highly-trained people. They reason that it's the other fellow or their circumstances that are at fault. They reason that their reactions, given their situation, are quite normal and natural. After all, aren't they being mistreated, misunderstood, not appreciated, and rejected? Isn't it normal to be upset and fight back in order to free yourself from the turmoil within you?

Many counselees say, "Anyone in my shoes would have reacted the way I did. Once I get out of this situation, my natural spirit of goodwill, good humor, friendliness, generosity, and unselfishness will return."

It is natural for people to become upset in the midst of trouble. Many people have been terribly mistreated since childhood. They have tasted of other people's selfishness. It is unbelievable how many people are subject to harsh, scornful, vicious, and inconsiderate treatment. Curiously enough, many individuals who have received terrible, shameful treatment in the past will themselves repeat the same treatment, or even worse, toward the people in their lives. They will attack or withdraw from anyone who resembles the past—retaliating, wallowing in self-pity, refusing to forgive. You would think that they would be more considerate and understanding of other people since they know what it is like to suffer from cruelty, harshness, and selfishness. Are they innocent victims of the past and therefore not accountable for their attitudes and conduct?

It is true that a troubled person calms down and is happier when the people and circumstances around him are pleasant. Many counselors reason, therefore, that it is the environment that causes the individual to be upset and to retaliate. They say that man is basically friendly, generous, selfless, and good. These qualities, some counselors say, will be present if the patient can find an environment that will allow the qualities to emerge, or if he can be taught to channel any aggressive tendencies into constructive activities.

But we have learned that trouble merely exposes man's natural tendency to react in an unfriendly, selfish, or bitter way. This basic evil nature is not so obvious when circumstances and the conduct of others are acceptable to an individual.

Help may be found only when people face the truth about themselves and then turn to God for the power to change in the midst of trouble. Their problems won't disappear; however, their reactions are changed. They soon discover that it is not a problem-free life they need, but a change of heart or to lean more firmly upon the God who has already changed their hearts.

The Results of a Changed Heart

The Spirit of God has a quieting effect on the body. Imagine responding to pressure, perplexities, persecution, and destruction with a quiet spirit. To experience quietness and peace is indeed a treasure.

On pages 96-97 I used a chart to compare Spirit-filled living with sin-controlled living. You can use it like a mirror, which reflects everything. First, look for the beauty and the healthy reflections that were obvious in your life today. But don't neglect any evidence of your sinful side; clean it up before you put down the mirror.

A wise, mature Christian wears clothing furnished by God. The Bible describes it in Colossians 3:12-17:

> *As God's chosen people, holy and dearly loved, clothe yourselves with*
>
> > *compassion,*
> >
> > *kindness,*
> >
> > *humility,*
> >
> > *gentleness*
> >
> > *and patience.*
> >
> > *Bear with each other*
> >
> > *and forgive whatever grievances you may have against one another. . . .*
> >
> > *put on love. . . .*
> >
> > *Let the peace of Christ rule in your hearts. . . .*
> >
> > *be thankful.*
> >
> > *Let the word of Christ dwell in you richly . . .*
> >
> > *teach*
> >
> > *and admonish one another with all wisdom . . .*
> >
> > *as you sing . . . with gratitude in your hearts to God.*
> >
> > *And whatever you do, whether in word or deed, do it all in the name of the Lord Jesus.*

13

Finding Peace from Stress

◆

When asked to address a high-school-age group, I spent some time off and on for several days pondering the content for my talk. After all, for years I've been out of touch (age 76) with teenagers, concentrating on speaking to adults.

We entered a room filled with about 200 teenagers sitting on the floor. It was bedlam in there. It seemed to me that they were all talking at once as loudly as they could. The group director stepped up to a lectern and shouted as loud as he could, "Let me have your attention! Attention, please! Let's be quiet! We have Dr. Brandt with us tonight. He has an important message for all of you."

Some members of the audience continued talking to each other. The director then shouted sternly, "I want you all to calm down and listen."

There was my opener. To this very moment I was struggling to find an approach to get their attention. I'm sure they all wondered what this old man could say to them.

Then I came up with an idea. I began, "I suspect that your director just made a request that some of you could not obey even if you wanted to. He asked you to calm down; I'll give you a reason why it is impossible for some of you to calm down." I then shared with them two lines from a play:

> There is a secret in his breast
> That will never let him rest.

Sure enough, I had their full attention. The stage was set to tell them a story. It was a lesson I learned when I was about 12 years old.

The High Cost of a Secret

It was raspberry season—my favorite berry. The neighbor down the street had several rows of raspberry bushes. I had strict orders to stay out of those bushes unless I had permission.

One day as I walked past those bushes I could see some big, juicy berries. There was no one around, so I slipped down a row of bushes and was surrounded by the luscious fruit. I helped myself to handfuls of them. What a treat! There was something about stolen fruit that made it taste extra good. The feel of those juicy berries going down my throat and settling in my stomach was delightfully satisfying. I couldn't have been more content.

Suddenly I heard someone yell, "What are you doing in there!" It was the lady who owned the bushes.

In my most sincere voice I replied, "I'm sorry. I won't ever do it again. Please don't tell my mother."

She wouldn't promise. I slipped away under her stern gaze.

Those berries in my stomach turned sour. They felt like a rock. My heart was pounding. I was worried.

Later, I heard my mother call me into the house. I was afraid and struggling for breath when I went in to face her. She was cheerful and relaxed and smiled at me and gave me a hug. She said, "I want you to go to the store."

I did, and it was a relief to get away from her. I brought the groceries home and she thanked me. That was all.

Later my mother called again. Could it be that the neighbor called? I went in, holding my breath. She said, "Supper is ready." My stomach hurt. Would I throw up if I ate? My dad asked, "Why don't you eat?"

"I'm eating, I'm eating," I stammered. I wasn't acting my normal self and I knew it. But I couldn't relax.

"Are you feeling good?" asked my mother.

"I'm fine," I whispered.

It was a horrible ordeal to sit at that table with my parents. If they knew what I had done, why didn't they tell me?

We watched TV most of the evening. Then my dad called me. He never called me unless something unusual was happening.

He simply said, "Go to bed."

I tossed and turned in my bed for a long time before I went into a troubled sleep. Breakfast time the next day was a terrible experience. I expected the neighbor to call at any moment. My mother was cheerful and friendly. If our neighbor had called my mother, she didn't tell me.

Later I was in our yard and I saw the neighbor walking toward our house. She came closer, closer, and closer. I hid behind the house so that she couldn't see me. I peeked around the corner and watched her walk past the house. Whe-e-ee, what a relief. But my stomach hurt. I couldn't relax.

And to this day, I never found out if my neighbor told my mother.

I was the architect of my own misery. As far as I knew, my mother had no knowledge of my behavior. But my secret came between my mother and me. Any effort on her part to be friendly toward me made me more uncomfortable. I felt sick and my stomach hurt.

The Bible says, "He who conceals his sins does not prosper, but whoever confesses and renounces them finds mercy" (Proverbs 28:13).

My sins were stealing and trying to cover it up.

You could have heard a pin drop in that teenage audience. I had stumbled upon a subject that was relevant to all of them.

My parting thought was, "A secret in your breast can keep you from rest." Not only do you create an invisible wall between you and someone else, but you also punish yourself. Your secret can cause your body to malfunction and cause physical pain.

Think a minute. What else can cause you pain and build invisible walls between you and someone you care about? How about . . .

- telling your parents you did your homework when in fact you didn't

- being jealous of someone else's good looks or talent

- acting rebellious because you must keep your room clean

Get the idea?

The response to that talk was amazing. The teenagers clapped enthusiastically when I finished. Since then I have shared the same message with other audiences of different ages and interests. Through an interpreter, I shared it with some primitive peoples who could not read or write and had no modern conveniences. They all got the message, too.

Secrets in your breast will never let you rest, and they will build invisible walls between yourself and other people.

How can you find rest? Like those teenagers, many of whom were restless and anxious, we must deal with our secrets, such as...

- something you did
- something you did not do
- some evil thought
- some emotional response

Do you have a secret in your breast that will never let you rest?

Fight or Flight

Sooner or later everyone tells themselves or other people to change their behavior. These are the words we use:

- Don't get excited!

- Calm down!
- Take it easy!
- Relax!

We use these words when we sense certain changes in our bodies that happen involuntarily:

- the heartbeat accelerates
- blood pressure increases
- muscles get tense
- digestion slows down or speeds up
- the mind becomes more alert
- emotions are stimulated

These bodily changes are labeled the "fight or flight" response. Another term in common use is "a state of adrenaline arousal." These changes are given a word: *stress*.

What Is Stress?

Experts who accept the theory of evolution explain that this response is a carryover from caveman days. When a caveman perceived something threatening or questionable, the "fight or flight" response kicked in automatically. After the caveman took action, his body returned to normal. Then he may have felt tired or even exhausted, depending on the energy he expended or the amount of stress he felt.

Nowadays we're told this prehistoric response is no longer appropriate. Civilized society places considerable restrictions on fighting, running, or explosive emotional demonstrations. But internally, the response remains.

The person who believes that God created this world would and should reject the prehistoric caveman explanation for stress. But we cannot deny the reality of stress; the symptoms are there. There are times when our bodies are mobilized involuntarily into a "fight or flight" pattern. Frequently, we are not in a position to flee or fight or explode. Those who don't know the biblical alternative are left stewing in their own juice. Clearly, they are unable to unwind from the daily stresses that can cause physiological damage.

Stress (the "fight or flight" response) is often an automatic response when a person perceives something threatening, dangerous, or evil. For example, let's say you are home alone reading the paper. You are reading an article that tells about several homes in your area that have been broken into recently. The article recommends that you lock all your doors and windows. At that moment, there is a knock on your door. You are not expecting anyone. So your body's alarm system kicks in automatically. You go to the front door cautiously and look through the peephole. It is a good friend. You calm down and your body returns to normal. This kind of stress response is healthy; it was a reasonable response to possible danger.

This kind of arousal is useful, for example, if an athlete gets "psyched up" for and during a game. It happens when a speaker prepares for and gives a speech. It can happen when you anticipate the arrival of a guest. A bride feels it on her wedding day. When these events are over, the body returns to normal and rests. These responses are called "good stress," or eustress.

If you worry all night after checking the keyhole, if the athlete remains psyched up all night, if the speaker stays keyed up all night, or if you are tense the whole time that your guest is with you, these responses are called "bad stress," or distress.

Stress is good only if it is short-lived. The ebb-and-flow effect is crucial to keep in mind.

Examples of Stress

Think about what happens to a child when he becomes excited—particularly when the excitement continues over a period of time. Six-year-old John begged his father to take him to the airport. One night his father said he would take him the next day. How excited John became! After tossing all night long in his sleep, he was awake bright and early. His body was so tense he could hardly sit through school. He talked about the airport and airplanes to his schoolmates, his teachers, the traffic officer on the corner, and to anyone else who would listen. About 5:00 that evening when his father drove up, he jumped up and down and clapped his hands.

"Dad's here! Dad's here!" He whipped out of the house to the car. Before his father could get out, he asked, "We're still going, aren't we, Dad? Aren't we?"

"Of course we're going," his dad replied. John ran back into the house with a shout. He only picked at his supper. His body did not require much food under the circumstances.

It was a thrilling evening watching airplanes take off and land and taxi back and forth. John's dad took him to a private airplane hangar and gave him a chance to explore a plane. Finally it was time to return home. John was fast asleep before the car left the airport parking lot. That's eustress.

✦ ✦ ✦

Jan looked forward to a date with the young man she thought was the most popular in the entire school. All day long she was keyed up. Her appetite disappeared. Even her memory became faulty. Her mother had given her a chore that she forgot about because of her excitement over the date. Neither could she study.

The doorbell rang. She heard his voice. Her excitement was at a high point. Her heart began to pound; her hands began to sweat. Her face became flushed. Making a last check of her makeup, she found that her hands were trembling. She experienced evident bodily changes that brought a pleasant sensation.

✦ ✦ ✦

Larry was elated. He had a date, and was doubling with a buddy and his girlfriend. He whistled and sang as he prepared to leave. His father had given him the car for the evening, and it had been no task at all to get it cleaned up for the occasion.

But when Larry arrived back home that night he was glum and disgusted. What had happened? His girl was late; the food bill was high; his friend and his friend's date got into an argument. The evening had been a flop. What a switch from the elation he had enjoyed as he was getting ready! His feelings had changed from pleasant to unpleasant. His bodily functions did not change. His eustress ended in distress.

✦ ✦ ✦

You can easily see from the preceding examples that emotions, whether pleasant or unpleasant, cause you to do something: jump up and down, sit and fret, or pace the floor. The bodily changes, however, must eventually return to normal for you to be comfortable and at ease. A child who has had an exciting day will drop into his bed at night in sheer exhaustion.

With adults, returning to balance is no less essential than for children. Even the most tender emotions, pleasant as they are, must subside, allowing bodily processes to revert to normal.

The Dangers of Stress

The fact that an emotion may be pleasant does not make the quest for it desirable. The thrill of driving at high speeds can be dangerous and deadly. The drive of sexual passion can throw you into deep trouble. Just the enjoyment of companionship with a friend can cause you to neglect important details and other relationships in life.

This statement by Dr. Hart sounds an important caution:

> A constant state of adrenaline arousal, although physically damaging, is often experienced as pleasant excitement and stimulation. And it is this that makes it most dangerous, because we can come to think of the arousal state as "normal" and to depend on the high it gives us to get anything accomplished.
>
> I believe there is corresponding spiritual danger. Becoming dependent on adrenaline arousal for the good feelings of life can create an association between spirituality and high arousal. *Don't*

confuse spirituality with adrenaline. In other words, one doesn't feel "spiritual" unless one is being stimulated by adrenaline arousal.

Many expressions of spirituality have become linked to adrenaline arousal, and this can be very harmful. A great many of the true saints of God have found their peak spiritual experiences in quietness and solitude. But many modern "saints" look for it only in exciting challenges or emotional catharsis.[1]

A certain amount of stress is good. Change makes life interesting. Most of us can handle one or two changes as they occur. Too much stress at once or a situation that is never dealt with can harm your physical or mental health. This is especially true if the stress is triggered by such responses as anger, resentment, hatred, stubbornness, selfishness, or rebellion. (These are sins.)

Such stress increases the possibility of a person becoming physically ill. Physicians are increasingly aware that stress contributes to the development of major disorders such as hypertension, strokes, diabetes, and even some forms of cancer. Stress is considered a primary factor in some digestive disorders, headaches, and nonspecific rashes.

Steven H. Applebaum has compiled this list of symptoms that warn you that you are experiencing too much stress. The following symptoms of stress are adequate indices since more dangerous distress can develop unless these initial symptoms are dealt with in the early stages:

1. General irritability, hyper excitation, or depression, usually associated with unusual aggressiveness or passive indolence, depending upon the personality style

2. Pounding of the heart and indicators of high blood pressure often due to stress

3. Dryness of the throat and mouth

4. Impulsive behavior or emotional instability

5. The overpowering urge to cry or run and hide

6. The inability to concentrate, flight of thoughts, and general disorientation

7. Feelings of unreality, weakness, or dizziness

8. Predilection that becomes fatigue, and loss of the joie de vivre [joy of living]

9. Floating anxiety—that is to say, people are afraid although they do not know exactly what they are afraid of

10. Emotional tension and alertness, feelings of being keyed up

11. Trembling and nervous tics

12. A tendency to be easily startled by small sounds

13. High-pitched nervous laughter

14. Stuttering and other speech difficulties that frequently are stress induced

15. Bruxism or grinding of the teeth

16. Insomnia, which usually is a consequence of being keyed up

17. Hyper mobility—often called hyperkinesia—an increased tendency to move without any reason or an inability to take a physically relaxed attitude

18. Sweating that becomes evident only under considerable stress by inspection of the skin

19. Frequent need to urinate, chronic diarrhea, indigestion, queasiness in the stomach and sometimes even vomiting that are all signs of disturbed gastrointestinal functions that may lead eventually to severe diseases of adaptation such as ulcerative colitis, peptic ulcer, spastic colon, and other maladies

20. Migraine headaches

21. Premenstrual tension or missed menstrual cycle

22. Pain in the back or neck

23. Excessive loss of appetite

24. Increased smoking

25. Increased use of legally prescribed drugs such as amphetamines and tranquilizers

26. Alcohol and drug addiction—like the phenomenon of overeating, increased and excessive consumption of alcohol and the use of various psychotrophic drugs is a common manifestation of exposure to stressors beyond individuals' natural endurance; in this case managers still are dealing with slight reactions that are considered to be deviations to which they resort, presumably to help them to forget the cause of the distress

27. Nightmares

28. Neurotic behavior

29. Psychoses

30. Accident proneness[2]

The psychological and physical problems caused by stress have become today's number-one health problem. Common medical estimates are that approximately 75 percent of all diseases have their origins in stress.

Some Sources of Stress

Martin was experiencing severe abdominal pain. He was having great difficulty swallowing food. After a long series of expensive tests, a stern-looking physician told him, "The tests show that your body is normal. All I can do is give you a tranquilizer that will relax your throat and some antacid pills that will relieve your stomach pain. The other option is for you to cease doing whatever you are doing that disturbs you."

Martin knew exactly what the physician meant. Deep inside, he was furious over a friend who had, in his opinion, betrayed a commitment to him.

✦ ✦ ✦

A lady in her late sixties was having asthma problems. It was controlled by medication. Her physician suspected the symptoms were stress-related and kept urging her to get some counseling. He was right; the woman had nursed a bitter, hostile grudge toward a husband who walked out on her 20 years ago.

✦ ✦ ✦

When a person transforms stress from a psychological conflict to a physical symptom, the resulting disorder is classified as a psychosomatic illness.

We tend to ignore the fact that we are comprised of body, mind, and spirit. These are usually divided up: the physician takes the body, the psychiatrist and the psychologist take the mind, and the minister gets the spirit. There is, however, a serious need to take a holistic approach to understanding human need.

People can learn to live with a surprising amount of mental anxiety and physical symptoms, as if they were anesthetized psychologically and physically. They can get to the point where they do not recognize discomfort anymore.

In our fast-paced, hurry-hurry society, stress is a word that describes many of us. Other words that come close are suspense, excitement, challenge, and competition.

The Value of Rest

Do you find it difficult to relax? Your body needs it. Besides, who said that a meaningful life must be fast-moving and exciting?

Even our Lord knew the value of rest. In Mark 6:31 Jesus told the disciples, "Come with me by yourselves to a quiet place and get some rest." And in Matthew 11:28,29, He said, "Come to me, all you who are weary and burdened, and I will give you rest. Take my yoke upon you and learn from me, for I am gentle and humble in heart, and you will find rest for your souls."

Jesus beckoned the tired and weary to come to

Him for rest. He related rest to a gentle and lowly heart. First Peter 3:4 tells us to seek "the unfading beauty of a gentle and quiet spirit, which is of great worth in God's sight."

To say the least, a gentle, lowly, quiet spirit comes highly recommended by Jesus Himself. The explanation that Jesus gives for urging us to seek such a heart is to find rest for our souls. A quiet heart results in a body at rest. A heart at peace is calm, restful, relaxed, untroubled, unafraid.

Does Jesus mean this should be your response when you lose your job, or when there is an accident, serious illness, pain, conflict in the family, divorce, death, a hurricane, or an earthquake?

He made the world, so He surely must have understood that these things would happen when He said, "I have told you these things, so that in me you may have peace. In this world you will have trouble. But take heart! I have overcome the world" (John 16:33).

14

Help for a Hard Journey

◆

Once you have accepted responsibility for your life, you will be tempted to backtrack, blame other people for your ups and downs, and leave your troubles and defeats at someone else's door. But don't become discouraged or misled. Temptation is something you hold in common with all people. And it, too, must be met with whatever resources you have with a willingness to be responsible for how you respond.

What is temptation? Smiley Blanton, a noted psychiatrist, offers a good definition:

> Every day of your life, no matter how sheltered you are, you face some choice in which the wrong action is so seductive, so plausible, so pleasurable that it takes a conscious effort of will to reject it. Temptation is universal, as old as the Garden of

Eden. Much of your happiness or unhappiness depends on your ability to handle it—instead of letting it handle you.[1]

Imagine that you are driving down a highway in a powerful car. The speed limit is 55 miles an hour. But the way is clear; no one is around; you know the car really purrs at 75. The temptation is to step on the gas.

Here's another example: As a Christian, you are committed to give of your income to the Lord, but the furniture is shabby and the sales are on. You are tempted to withhold your tithe "just this one time."

Or, you have promised to spend the evening with your family. A fellow worker, however, has two tickets to the deciding ball game of a crucial series. He wants you to go with him. You are tempted to go.

Subtle Situations

Temptation does not always appear as a terrible, undesirable evil that you clearly shouldn't do. There will be times when you are greatly tempted by something subtle that you want to do but know you shouldn't. (Or it could be the reverse—something that you should do but don't want to.)

At the moment of temptation, giving in may seem so right. An impulsive purchase that will later wreck the household budget may seem so right at first. To dish out a strong punishment to someone may seem so right in the passion of emotion. So right—except you have to remember that your heart can be so deceitful.

Mrs. Craig, expecting guests, was cleaning the house when the telephone rang. Some friends were meeting downtown for lunch. They wanted to know if she could join them.

"I'd love to meet you, but you know my husband. He's fussy about the way the house looks for company."

"It's just a quick lunch."

"Well, I don't know."

It was a difficult decision. She certainly wanted to join her friends. But should she suit herself or please her husband? She faced temptation.

Mrs. Van Waggoner and her neighbor were golfing. They were about to tee off for the third hole when two men approached the women and asked if they could play through. Mrs. Van Waggoner and her partner readily agreed. But before the men went on, one suggested that the women join them in their game. The women looked at each other. Mrs. Van Waggoner had never faced this situation before. She was quite uneasy about the suggestion, but her neighbor said OK before she could think much about it.

The men proved to be cheerful company—and most attentive. Mrs. Van Waggoner's partner teed up her ball for her, pulled her cart, and helped her improve her iron shots. Perhaps he was a bit too friendly, yet she enjoyed the attention.

After the game, the foursome drank iced tea in the clubhouse. As they were about to leave, Mrs. Van Waggoner's partner suggested they have lunch together at a nice little restaurant he knew of. She was tempted—the morning had been so pleasant. To refuse took a definite act of her will, but she did it.

At home she was upset that she had responded so warmly to this strange man. The morning had been filled with temptation, and she wondered what to tell her husband. She found out—as you probably have—

that temptation can pop up in the most unexpected places and in the most unusual ways. It can make you aware of desires that take you by surprise.

The Bible says,

> When tempted, no one should say, "God is tempting me." For God cannot be tempted by evil, nor does he tempt anyone; but each one is tempted when, by his own evil desire, he is dragged away and enticed. Then, after desire has conceived, it gives birth to sin; and sin, when it is full-grown, gives birth to death. Don't be deceived, my dear brothers (James 1:13-16).

The temptations that bother most people are not those that would clearly lead into sin. Not many people struggle hard with the temptation to steal. But the semi-visible testings are something else. It was not perfectly clear that it was wrong for Mrs. Craig to drop her house-cleaning to join her friends downtown.

Each person has his own personal, private standards that he has chosen to live by; to fall short is to cause himself personal anxiety. Because Mrs. Craig had set for herself a goal of getting the house cleaned, it is likely she would not have enjoyed the luncheon.

The apostle Paul said, "Whatever you believe about these things keep between yourself and God. Blessed is the man who does not condemn himself by what he approves" (Romans 14:22).

Everyone faces tempting circumstances constantly. While I was writing this book, I was tempted to lay down my pen and attend a professional golf tournament that was playing in town. To take a break might have been all right, but I had committed myself to a deadline for finishing the manuscript. I resisted the temptation every day but one.

It was an exciting tournament. My enjoyment of it, however, was dampened by the fact that I had left an unfinished task behind. I constantly chastised myself afterward for allowing myself to succumb to temptation.

Preparing for the Test

In advance of a temptation you must make up your mind not to yield to it. Nevertheless, when temptation comes, you must reaffirm your previously made decision, and this will require a definite act of the will.

Character is forged from encounters and situations that tempt you to do wrong. The erring attraction is always present. Paul reminded the Corinthians, "So, if you think you are standing firm, be careful that you don't fall!" (1 Corinthians 10:12).

It is good for you to compare notes with other people. You may feel that no one else faces the same temptations you do. The counselor hears this constantly: The counselee struggles to tell of his temptations. At times, he overcomes them; at times, he fails. In telling his story he feels that he is revealing something that no one else has ever experienced.

Mr. E., a deacon and sincere Christian, cannot keep his eyes off a woman who recently joined the church.

Mrs. G. is seized with a sudden impulse to slip that nice little knickknack into her purse.

Mrs. H. would like to scratch out her neighbor's eyes because the neighbor won't keep her children out of Mrs. H.'s yard.

The person who thinks he is the only one to face a particular kind of temptation is inclined to justify yielding to it. "You would make allowances for my mean disposition if you knew what I have to put up with at home," a woman will say, as if there were no other cantankerous husband in the world but her own—and so the story of temptation goes. But Paul said,

> *No temptation has seized you except what is common to man. And God is faithful; he will not let you be tempted beyond what you can bear. But when you are tempted, he will also provide a way out so that you can stand up under it (1 Corinthians 10:13).*

Taking the way of escape is your choice, and God is always ready to help you make that choice. But you must remember that your decision on whether or not to yield comes in the face of a wrong action that is so seductive, so plausible, so pleasurable that it takes a conscious act of the will to reject it. The desire to do what you want to do, even though it is wrong, is very strong.

Jesus gave us a strange-sounding formula: "If anyone would come after me, he must deny himself and take up his cross and follow me. For whoever wants to save his life will lose it, but whoever loses his life for me will find it" (Matthew 16:24,25).

All people are tempted to please only themselves, but the pathway to inner peace is to lose yourself in God's way, to follow Him and do His will at all costs. Inner peace comes to those who seek first the kingdom of God and His righteousness (Matthew 6:33), to those who "pursue righteousness, [and] godliness" (1 Timothy 6:11). To enjoy God's peace, you must "follow after the things which make for peace" (Romans 14:19 KJV).

When Temptation Pursues You

Temptations will pursue you even when you seek to determine in what, or in whom, you will put your faith. If you choose the Bible as your guide, there will be those who will try to divert you from it. But God has His "persuaders," too. If you reject the Bible, there will be those who will challenge your decision and seek to "tempt" you to return to God's Word and the things of the Lord. For example, many churches conduct weekly calling programs persuading people to attend Sunday school in order to study the Bible.

In my early twenties I went through a period of rejecting the church, the Bible, and anyone who held to them. It was easy to find people who encouraged me in my rejection. I read articles and books by educators and psychologists who said that man was capable of taking care of himself without crutches such as church and the Bible. Scientific research, they said, would save us.

But others who knew me and who had been helped by the church, the Lord, and a study of His Word were not content to let me rest in this decision. They called on me frequently and exerted great effort to get me to reconsider.

After some years I returned to church and renewed my faith in God and the Bible. During college and graduate school I purposed in my heart, by faith, to use the Bible as my standard for conduct and for evaluating what I heard or read. From that point onward the Bible was never on trial with me, but the book I was reading or the professor's lecture was. Just as my friends in the church were not content to let my earlier rejection go unchallenged, so my fellow students and professors did not let my latter decision to accept the Bible as my guide go unchallenged.

"How can you possibly explain putting your faith in the Bible and at the same time be a student of psychology?" they would ask. They tempted me greatly. I wanted my friends and professors to respect and like me. But to have their full respect meant to put my faith where theirs was—in the idea that man is in a process of evolution, in the belief that with our own hands we can build a world of peace.

They never let me forget that every person has a right to choose how he will spend his life and that it is not right for one to impose his standards on another. But as I understood it, the kind of life a person lived was not a matter of his own opinion. For everyone would be judged someday, and the standard for judgment was the Bible. Holding to such a view, I stood alone. How great was the temptation to be like the people around me!

Today there are writers and speakers, some of them ministers and seminary professors, who are not convinced that the Bible is entirely the Word of God. To consider what they say is to court temptation to give up your reliance on the Bible. Something you read, hear on the radio or in a speech or in a conversation, or see on television can tempt you to deviate from what you believe. This will be true whatever course you follow. Having chosen a way for yourself, you will be tempted incessantly to turn from it. And among those tempting you will be people you admire.

Recently a college student came to me with a question that troubled him: "Some of the finest people I know are not Christians. They openly spurn the Bible. Yet they seem to be happy and get along well with other people. Some of the leading people in our church are much harder to get along with and do not appear to be as happy as those who are not Christians. If God's way is the only way to peace, then why are these non-Christians peaceful and these Christians not?"

That's a good question. One's conduct does have an impact on others. This young man's faith was being shaken by the conduct of professing Christians. According to his observations, it did not seem to matter if he did not place his faith in Christ and God's Word.

His observations were correct, but you cannot allow yourself to become confused by observing others. The Bible says, "Do not consider his appearance or his height, for I have rejected him. The LORD does not look at the things man looks at. Man looks at the outward appearance, but the LORD looks at the heart" (1 Samuel 16:7).

As a counselor, I see many people who are woefully unhappy individuals, yet they never give any outward indication of it. A person's outward behavior does not always give a measure of what is going on inside him. We cannot judge a person by what happens to him. The Bible says that God "causes his sun to rise on the evil and the good, and sends rain on the righteous and the unrighteous" (Matthew 5:45).

We should be careful about making judgments based on the success or lack of success we see in the lives of other people. Paul said, "Therefore let us stop passing judgment on one another. Instead, make up your mind not to put any stumbling block or obstacle in your brother's way" (Romans 14:13).

Whom Will You Trust?

Where will you place your faith? In the conduct of man? In the words or writings of some individual? Or in God and His Word? You must make this choice alone and then face the ceaseless temptations to change your choice.

Remember the definition offered earlier: Your decision comes in the face of a wrong action that is so seductive, so plausible, so pleasurable that it takes a conscious act of the will to reject it. In the college student's case, when questions arose about the negative conduct of professing Christians, it seemed reasonable to turn away from the Bible and to take the viewpoint followed by those who appeared happier. This young man had to make his choice.

Now it is my privilege to "tempt" you with this viewpoint: The Bible is your sure guide to peace.

We know that the person who disobeys the rules of health will be sick, whether he likes it or not. Likewise, the person who violates biblical principles will be unhappy, whether he appears to be or not. We say this by faith. But we say it by experience, too. The unhappy, tense, anxious, miserable person who comes to a counselor for help is usually knowingly or unknowingly violating some biblical principle.

How do you approach the God who can give you inner peace? Hebrews 11:6 says, "Without faith it is impossible to please God, because anyone who comes to him must believe that he exists and that he rewards those who earnestly seek him." Back in Hebrews 11:1, we read that "faith is being sure of what we hope for and certain of what we do not see."

You must approach God by faith. You must trust Him fully, with your mind set on Him and His ways. And when you do, you will know peace: "You will keep in perfect peace him whose mind is steadfast, because he trusts in you. Trust in the LORD forever, for the LORD, the LORD, is the Rock eternal" (Isaiah 26:3,4).

As you trust God, He will give you assurance that you are on the right path. But trials, troubles, conflicts, other viewpoints, and unexpected failures on your part and on the part of other people you admire will challenge your evidence and throw you back on faith alone. A combination of faith and temptation will make your choice of the Bible as your guide a difficult one to maintain.

The Challenge and the Reward

Let me "tempt" you to make a one-year test of studying and applying to your life the truths that you find in the Bible. Now to study, to ponder, to test what the Bible says takes time. After all, a student who chooses a career in psychology spends four years just getting his bachelor's degree. At that point, he is only a beginner in the field. Likewise, it takes time to test the guidance the Bible offers to those who trust God, its author.

Romans 12:2 tells us, "Do not conform any longer to the pattern of this world, but be transformed by the renewing of your mind. Then you will be able to test and approve what God's will is—his good, pleasing and perfect will."

This verse implies your knowledge of God's Word and love for and obedience to that knowledge. There is no simple, easy approach to inner peace. It is a struggle with a starting point based on simple faith, with many temptations along the way to draw you aside, on a pathway that today is rejected by many serious, dedicated, sincere people.

The reward is still there for those who take God's way in spite of the difficulties. And there is help along the route. Prayer is the gateway to getting this help from God:

Let us then approach the throne of grace with confidence, so that we may receive mercy and find grace to help us in our time of need (Hebrews 4:16).

> *Do not be anxious about anything, but in everything, by prayer and petition, with thanksgiving, present your requests to God. And the peace of God, which transcends all understanding, will guard your hearts and your minds in Christ Jesus (Philippians 4:6,7).*

Jesus said, "You may ask me for anything in my name, and I will do it" (John 14:14). And He followed that with these words, "If you love me, you will obey what I command" (John 14:15).

If you want your prayers for help answered, become familiar with the commands of God in the Bible. Verbalize your longings before God, then wait to see what He will do. If you have asked according to His will (that is, if you have prayed with the desire that *His* will may be done), you will have what you asked for. It is yours if it fits into God's plan. And remember that His ways are not necessarily your ways (Isaiah 55:8,9). But also, His ways are not grievous or burdensome (1 John 5:3).

Your challenge is to accept the Bible as your guide and to obey God's commands fully. If you do, you will find that the Bible is a mirror in which you see yourself as you really are. And when you see yourself, what you do is *still* up to you. You can correct what ought to be corrected. But you will be tempted to look away and forget what you saw (James 1:23-25). And in looking away you will soon become absorbed in counterattractions that will not let you return for a second look.

If by faith you go God's way, you will find inner peace along the path as well as at the end of the road.

A past president of the United States offered this advice:

The sum of the whole matter is this, that our civilization cannot survive materially unless it be redeemed spiritually. It can be saved only by becoming permeated with the spirit of Christ and being made free and happy by the practices which spring out of that spirit. Only thus can discontent be driven out and all the shadows lifted from the road ahead.

Here is the final challenge to our churches, to our political organizations, and to our capitalists—to everyone who fears God or loves his country. Shall we not all earnestly cooperate to bring in this new day?[2]

✦ ✦ ✦

Whoever would love life and see good days must keep his tongue from evil and his lips from deceitful speech. He must turn from evil and do good; he must seek peace and pursue it. For the eyes of the Lord are on the righteous and his ears are attentive to their prayer, but the face of the Lord is against those who do evil (1 Peter 3:10-12).

Notes

Introduction—Before You Begin
1. Karl Menninger, *Whatever Became of Sin?* (New York: Hawthorne Books, 1973), p. 14.
2. Ibid., 91.

Chapter 2—How Thoughts and Feelings Can Hurt You
1. O. Spurgeon English, "The Emotional Cause of Symptoms" (Lititz, PA: Youth Club Service Hour, Lititz Church of the Brethren, n.d.), brochure printed by Sandoz Pharmaceuticals of New York.
2. Mrs. English, "Pain with a Purpose," a five-page self-published tract, n.d.
3. S.I. McMillen, *None of These Diseases* (Waco, TX: Word Books, n.d.), 64-65.
4. Ibid., 73-74.

Chapter 3—The Law of Sin
1. Henry Drummond, *The Greatest Thing in the World* (London: Collins Press, 1887), 32-36.
2. *The Concise Columbia Dictionary of Quotations* (New York: Columbia University Press, 1990), Microsoft Bookshelf 1992, s.v. "Drink: Drunkenness is nothing but voluntary madness..."
3. Ibid., s.v. "Drink: Drunkenness is temporary suicide."
4. "7 in 100 Charged with DUI Go to Jail," *Palm Beach Post*, Dec. 31, 1992, 1A.

Chapter 6—Sick or Sinful?
1. Hobart O. Mowrer, "Sin, the Lesser of Two Evils," *The American Psychologist*, May 1960, 301-04.
2. Ibid.
3. Ibid.
4. Ibid.
5. Ibid.

Chapter 7—The Missing Link
1. Hobart O. Mowrer, "Sin, the Lesser of Two Evils," *The American Psychologist*, May 1960, 304.
2. W. Phillip Keller, *The Good Shepherd and His Sheep* (Grand Rapids, MI: Zondervan Publishing House, 1978), 128-29.
3. *The Concise Columbia Dictionary of Quotations* (New York: Columbia University Press, 1990), Microsoft Bookshelf 1992, s.v. "Suffering: God had one son on earth..."

Chapter 8—How to Deal with Your Anger
1. *The American Heritage Dictionary* (Boston: Houghton Mifflin, 1987), Microsoft Bookshelf 1992, s.v. "an•ger."
2. Kenneth Appel and Edward Strecker, *Discovering Ourselves* (New York: Macmillan, 1962), 114-15.
3. *The Concise Columbia Dictionary of Quotations* (New York: Columbia University Press, 1990), Microsoft Bookshelf 1992, s.v. "Anger: No man can think clearly when..."
4. "Anger Hurts As Much As Obesity, Cigarettes," *Palm Beach Post*, Dec. 13, 1990, 1A.
5. "Expressing Anger Is What Kills," *Palm Beach Post*, Dec. 13, 1990, 1A.

Chapter 11—Perfect Love Eliminates Fear
1. "Researchers Dissect Our Fears," *Palm Beach Post*, Jul. 1, 1993, 1D.

Chapter 12—Enjoying the Spirit of Life in Christ
1. "Areopagitica," *Complete Poetry of Selected Prose of John Milton* (New York: Random House, 1950), 677.

Chapter 13—Finding Peace from Stress
1. Archibald O. Hart, *Adrenalin and Stress* (Waco, TX: Word Books, 1986), 58.
2. Steven H. Applebaum, *Stress Management Aspen System* (Rockville, MD: Aspen Publishers, 1981), 77-78.

Chapter 14—Help for a Hard Journey
1. Smiley Blanton, "How to Handle Temptation," *Reader's Digest*, May 1961, 188.
2. Woodrow Wilson, "The Road Away from Evolution," *Atlantic Monthly*, 1923.